The Bridge Never Crossed...

A Survivor's Search for Meaning

by

George A. Burk

Captain, USAF (Retired)

Science & Humanities Press

PO Box 7151

Chesterfield, MO 63006-7151

www.sciencehumanitiespress.com

The Bridge Never Crossed
        A Survivor's Search for Meaning

Graphics Credits:
The cover was derived from stock photographs in the IMSI
Masterclips and Nova Art Explosion Collections.

Copies of newspaper clippings are included with the kind
permission of the *Sonoma Index-Tribune*, Sonoma, CA

ISBN 1-888725-16-8
Library of Congress Catalog Card Number: 98-89869
First Printing, January, 1999

Science &
Humanities Press
PO Box 7151
Chesterfield, MO 63006-7151
(636) 394-4950
www.sciencehumanitiespress.com

To: Chris —
It was a great pleasure
meeting you —
thank for your service
God Bless you —
God Bless our troops!

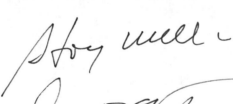

The Bridge
Never Crossed...

Stay well —

George Bush

Mark 9: 49-50; 71-24
1 Chron 4:10

Dedication

To the memory of my mother, Willa Burk,
whose support, love, positive energy,
and humor served as an inspiration to me.

I give all the praise for my life being saved to God and His working through the many people who have helped me. All that I have today I owe to Him and without Him in my life, I would fall.

God saved my life for a purpose: to help others, to send a message of faith and hope, and to inspire people to pursue their dreams and live each day to its fullest.

It is my hope and prayer this story has accomplished this purpose.

———◆—◆◈◆——

"…but we also rejoice in our sufferings, because we know that suffering produces perseverance; perseverance, character; and character, hope. And hope does not disappoint us, because God has poured out his love into our hearts by the Holy Spirit, whom He has given us."

Romans 5:3-5

Contents

Acknowledgments

*"People always remember two things—who kicked them
when they were down, and who helped them up."*
Harvey MacKay

Many people have contributed their time and energy to
help me regain my health and towards the completion of
this book through their positive influence, commitment
and caring.

My wife, Olga, who supported and encouraged me to
resurrect my manuscript and insisted that I complete the
book. Her support is even more meaningful in the context
of her love and respect for me as her husband.

The mother of my three children who experienced
firsthand the results of the plane crash and the havoc it
brought to the families whose husbands and fathers
perished. She stayed the course when an easier choice
could have been made. Often times, it is the families of
burn survivors who suffer the most.

The man who saved my life and his wife, John and Pearl
Davieau. John found me on fire outside of the wreckage
and extinguished the flames. Without him, I would have
burned to death.

My primary care physician, Dr. Wellford W. Inge. When
prevailing medical wisdom suggested he make me as
comfortable as possible since my demise was certain, he
never gave up on me and never let me quit. His
professionalism, commitment and love are part of the
reason I am alive today. To Doctor Tom Newsome, Doctor
Hugh Peterson and Doctor John Bostwick.

The medical staff on duty at Hamilton AFB, California,
May 4, 1970, for their efforts to reduce my discomfort,

help my family, and "find" the C-141 Starlifter which transported me to San Antonio, Texas.

The Air Force flight crew and flight nurse who diverted from Travis AFB, California, Monday, May 4, 1970, and flew me and a planeload of Vietnam veterans and burn survivors to San Antonio, Texas.

My ICU nurses, Captains Myra Peche and Sheri McGhee, Mrs. Wolfe, "Granny," Mr. Allen and all the staff at the burn unit, Brooke Army Medical Center for their professionalism, compassion and love.

To the families of the men who perished in the crash. I hope I have lived my life in a manner that honors your husbands, fathers and my friends.

Colonel Jim Neff and his wife Fletch, Major General Paul Stoney and scores of others, in and out of the Air Force, who gave me another chance to work and continue my life. Without them, my path after leaving the hospital may have been totally different.

Two men with whom I shared time in the burn unit and who have been a significant influence on my life, Roger Paulmeno and Chuck Nowlin. They served their country with distinction and honor and continue to be a source of pride and inspiration to me.

Mom and Dad, who loved me unconditionally. Mom was always there for me and my family. I love and miss them both! My three children Walter, Kimberly, and Scott Burk, my grandchildren, Walter Jr., Jackie, Allie, Jonathan, Tyler, and Holly, and my Godson, James Kobolt. I hope my story will inspire them and let them know what happened to "Pap-pap." My sister Billie Ann and brother-in-law Jim Myers, Tom and Miriam Parrish, Bud and Dolores Parrish, Lance and Arlyne Parrish, and Dick and Mary Pat Parrish for their faith, love, and support. To my aunt, Anne Parrish, who loved me like a son, made a special trip to see me in the hospital and baked me her special pineapple upside down cakes.

Colonel John Arms, USMCR (Ret), Colonel Rex Williams, USMCR (Ret), and Colonel Danny Hundley, USMCR, whose leadership and encouragement provided me the opportunity to succeed.

Jimmy Curran, Larry Smith, Bill Wekenborg, Jim Arnold, Helen Campbell, Joe Howard, Mike Simmons, Jeff DeBell, Scott Hoch, Rick Fagan, Pat Mays, and scores of other Fire and Life Safety personnel who helped me learn, grow and share my messages to personnel around the country.

Dr. John Dawson, President Emeritus, President Stanley Caine, Coach Greg Arbaugh, Henry Mensing, Coach Buck Riley and the staff at Adrian College. I thank them for their love, support and dedication to excellence in the classroom, on the athletic field and on the basketball floor.

Mr. and Mrs. Orville Merillat, founders of Merillat Woodworking Company. They made such an impact on my life that words cannot adequately describe my love, respect and admiration for them. They both really do walk the talk in thought, word and deed.

Don Zink, who passed away in November 1996, and his wife Ginny. Don was a man of great courage, was respected by many, had a contagious smile and a great sense of humor. It is hard to believe it has been over thirty years since those summers playing ball and when I used to carry Shelly around on my shoulders. Also, Ray and Mary Larned, Jerry and Beverly Pate. I cherish their friendship.

My friend, Larry Francouer. As I write this in October 1998, Larry is continuing the good fight against a terrible disease. The dignity and integrity in which he and his wife Judy have faced this battle is a source of inspiration to all of their friends. Larry is a great friend and one of my heroes.

Les Griffin and Floyd Huggins for their friendship and counsel.

Dr. Bud Banis and his wife, Lois, whose commitment, energy, and caring attitude in editing and producing this book was invaluable. Without Bud's guidance, this book might not have been published.

Other close friends, clients, students and people too numerous to name individually who have also been sources of learning, support and inspiration in my life's journey and in the writing of *The Bridge Never Crossed*.

Thank you all for being there for me.

Foreword

by Colonel and Mrs. James M. Neff, USAF (Ret)

The George Burk of today is the creation of a miracle. To have known him over the years has been a great privilege for my wife and myself. Courage, confidence, patriotism, love for fellowman and life define George. Only a chosen few could have endured his experiences and only a few of those would have retained this man's love of life.

I first met George at Danang Air Base, Vietnam. He was a young Air Traffic Control Officer—tall, robust, and athletic. His concern then was to understand a very complex, high density air traffic environment and take measures to insure safe and efficient control. Handling fighter/bombers, airlift and cargo aircraft interspersed with civil and military VIP traffic was no piece of cake—especially so during inclement weather and enemy mortar fire.

He so favorably impressed me, that I made certain he joined my Air Traffic Control staff at Hamilton AFB. It was there his life was changed forever.

In a few short minutes his robust, athletic body was reduced to a burned and broken mass by an aircraft crash and fire. George, however, remained within the charred body and bid farewell to the others as they crossed over the bridge.

For weeks, in the Burn Center at Ft. Sam Houston, his life balanced on a thin line. A young Army surgeon and his team worked day and night to keep George alive. Finally, we were advised that he was out of the woods and we could see him. My wife and I drove to San Antonio and were met at the hospital by his surgeon. He prepared us for what we would see; it was not pleasant. The voice and optimism were there—we knew it was

5

George. We heard of the encouragement he gave, to get with it and live, and how much good it was actually doing his fellow patients.

As we were leaving, I asked the surgeon how he could stand up under the pressures of working with these patients, day in and day out. He smiled and said, "You have to have a George Burk once in awhile." He was right. We all need a George Burk.

As you read George's story, you will admire and respect the internal strength of this man.

Colonel and Mrs. James M. Neff, USAF (Ret), August, 1998

Captain George Burk with Colonel & Mrs. James Neff.

Prologue

Let me introduce myself. My name is Captain George Burk, USAF (Ret). It's only now, after nearly thirty years, that I can reflect on a period of my life which was both tragic and inspirational. Yet try as I may, I still cannot logically account for my humble presence upon this planet. I can only be thankful to a power greater than all earthly powers and to those who befriended, helped and guided me.

Sometimes during the darker moments of my reflection I wonder why, apart from so many fine colleagues, my life was spared to endure the sequence of events and horrendous consequences that began that morning.

It was a West Coast spring morning that dawned foggy and overcast like so many other Northern California spring mornings. It was May 4, 1970, and there was never a hint or omen in that salt-laden sea mist billowing westward from the steamy Pacific Ocean to herald that day which so dramatically changed the remainder of my life and the lives of so many others.

After surviving an event as horrifying as a plane crash, one might spend considerable time and energy reviewing every detail of that day to determine if a safer path or course of action might have been taken. Another course or choice which would alter events; a different decision to avoid the physical and emotional pain and psychological torture of burns and disfigurement which left me, at its worst, wishing I would die.

Well, I didn't die, and my life since the crash has been full of adventure, excitement and, yes, even a few disappointments.

God has blessed me with a second chance at life, to travel and share my journey with others and have family and friends who love me.

Given pain, we can make the choice to wallow in our grieving, or we can take what is left to us as a gift, and build from there. Like so many others, I found in my pain a new source of determination and a new beginning. I feel I am a stronger person for it, and I am grateful for what I have learned.

Chapter One: My Journey Begins

"Success is not a destination that you ever reach. Success is the quality of the journey."   **Jennifer James**

Our takeoff down the fog-shrouded runway was uneventful.

Little did any of us know what we were to experience over the next terror-filled minutes. The cabin interior was cold and damp, consequences of the fog, low clouds and light rain which was falling; all was quiet except for the monotonous drone of the engines.

As I placed my head on my arms to take a short nap, a crackling sound from the cabin window next to Ken Yarger's left shoulder startled me from my half-sleep state. One-by-one, Ken, Fred Adams, and I stared at the window where a small horizontal line suddenly appeared midway up the glazing. The line stretched the length of the window. Although the window itself did not appear to be in any danger of blowing out, I suggested to Ken he make his way forward and inform Pappy, our crew chief, that we may have a problem.

Ken unbuckled his seat belt, slid over to the aisle and made his way to the front of the cabin to alert the crew. Within a matter of seconds, a strange whining tone, low at first then gradually increasing in pitch, rapidly filled the cabin. The sound lasted only a few seconds then was followed by a loud explosion which ripped through the aircraft. The sound of a fierce explosion and the feeling of the plane shuddering as it decompressed was unlike any noise I had ever experienced in my life! As the nose of the aircraft pitched and spiraled violently downward, all the cabin windows cracked and were blown-out! Seconds later, paper, seat cushions, small briefcases and other unsecured items swirled furiously around the open cabin and were rapidly sucked out of the open windows. The instant decompression pained my ears and above me, droplets of condensation appeared in the cabin then disappeared with equal rapidity.

Quickly glancing at the port then starboard wings, I noticed both engines were on fire and sputtering erratically, the propellers turning in the downdraft. Suddenly, a loud metallic ping-like noise rattled from the tail section of the aircraft, an indication that the rudder cables had severed.

The aircraft, pitching, yawing, and rolling with increased intensity and turbulence created a deafening noise in the plane's cabin. The noise was so loud, it literally blocked all conscious thoughts! At the moment of decompression, I was looking down the aisle towards the rear of the plane. Sitting on an aisle seat, just beyond an arched doorway and seated forward, was one of my best friends, Major Bob Ward. When the plane decompressed, we were thrust downward with such force that Bob's left leg was thrown upward.

As the plane continued to pitch, yaw and roll wildly in a downward angle, I unbuckled my seat belt, stood up, turned and placed my hands on the bulkhead doorway to brace myself. Ken Yarger was coming back up the aisle towards me, trying to return to his seat. His blue Air Force raincoat was spread horizontally from his armpits due to the severe wind sheer. Ken had a frightened and disbelieving look in his eyes which seemed as large as silver dollars. He passed me without comment, returned to his seat and assumed the crash position. This was real, and we knew it; death was soon coming to take us all away!

Surveying the damage in the cockpit, the destruction before me was unbelievable. I saw more open sky than airplane! Pappy was standing in the doorway holding the cabin door handle in the full down position desperately trying to keep the stairwell from tearing away at the fuselage. The front section of the cockpit lay split open like a nutshell, while the top part of the canopy was peeled back and flapped in the wind. The entire left side of the cockpit had disappeared.

The instrument panel, with its wiring, lay strewn across Colonel Shelton's lap while his co-pilot's steering yoke vibrated wildly back and forth and from side-to-side. It was obvious Colonel Shelton had lost control of the aircraft. The pilot, Captain Chuck Robinson, lay slumped forward, decapitated. It was all surreal. While the plane continued its descent and violently pitched, yawed and rolled, I turned around to my right and stumbled back to my seat. The shock of seeing the absolute and complete devastation of the cockpit, Robinson decapitated, and the decompression temporarily paralyzed my mind, and a sick, queasy feeling hit the pit of my stomach like a fireball. I instinctively knew my life was about to end.

After buckling my seat belt, I placed something in my lap, a pillow or small blanket blown free during the decompression and instinctively leaned forward and assumed the crash position. Above the wind shear and with the engines sputtering loudly in the background, I heard Fred Adams scream, "My God, we're not gonna make it!" As the plane continued its downward path, my last conscious thoughts were of my family. My mind strangely dredged up the hope that my insurance policies were current to provide sufficient funds for my wife and a proper education for my three children.

The impact, followed by the crunching sounds of metal shearing, bending and breaking is still vivid in my mind today. The force of the crash thrust my head forcibly against the back of my bulkhead seat. As the plane turned, twisted and collapsed like a telescope, then stopped abruptly, it threw my torso forward, and I struck my head across the table in front of me.

After all movement ceased, I unbuckled my seatbelt, stood in a half-erect position and turned to my left in my attempt to get out of the plane.

"C'mon Fred, let's get the hell out of here!" I shouted to Fred Adams.

I think Fred was dead before the impact.

Then one horrific sensation engulfed me as a large flash of super-heated air from a fireball shot through the plane. It was as if someone had dumped a large bucket of scalding hot water all over me. At that instant, everything went blank and I awoke outside the burning wreckage, face down in the dirt, with the plane and trees burning around me.

As a result of the impact and post-crash fire, my range of injuries included a four-inch compressed fracture of the spine, two cracked vertebrae, three severed vertebrae, four cracked ribs, a separation of my left shoulder, skull fracture, a broken nose, two broken bones in my neck, and burns over sixty-five percent of my body. Thirty-five percent of the burns were third-degree, and the fingers on my left hand received fourth-degree burns, meaning the flesh was burned to the bone. The only parts of my body surface not burned were my chest, upper back and groin.

The ninety days spent in the Intensive Care Unit (ICU) and my eighteen months in the hospital were long and arduous for me and my family. I required a ventilator to assist my breathing, suffered two collapsed lungs, double lobar pneumonia, and numerous blood stream and other life-threatening infections.

Chapter Two: Takeoff!

"You cannot escape your life issues. Why not transform them?"   **Eric Allenbaugh**

Peering through the partially opened curtains in our bathroom window, a white curtain of fog and light rain swirled around the large tree in the front yard.

"Not exactly prime flying weather. Maybe clear above cloud level," I thought, then dismissed my speculation, shaved and took a shower.

It was 0645 hours, and my routine was a bit "behind the power curve" considering the negative weather conditions for our scheduled takeoff at 0800 hours.

Dressed in my summer weight uniform and my packing completed, I looked in at my sleeping children then grabbed my blue uniform jacket and kissed my wife goodbye.

Out in the carport, I loaded my B-4 bag and briefcase into the trunk of my Austin-Healy Sprite, backed out of the driveway and headed slowly along the road toward Base Operations at the airfield. It was 0710 hours, and the fog and light rain became more dense as I approached the airfield.

The Operational Analysis mission our team was to complete was at Fairchild AFB near Spokane, Washington. It would be another routine trip as a member of the Air Traffic Control and Maintenance Evaluation Team. The responsibilities of my position required me to travel many times during that eighteen-month assignment. By then, learning curves were far behind and work content had become mundane, perhaps somewhat repetitive. My occupational satisfaction graph had taken a dip. In fact, although difficult to conceive it when my assignment began, the job was becoming a bit boring. But this day, anticipation rushed through my head as I eagerly looked to the future.

After one more trip, my assignment at Hamilton would end, taking me to greener pastures and a new duty station. Within the next two months Okinawa, Japan, would be our new home for the next three years. New sights and cultures and a fresh scenario for my wife and kids. Above all, the new job presented a fresh challenge. At last, my horizon had been extended. My eagerness to arrive in Okinawa was exceeded only by my impatience with the timeline of our pending trip.

Arriving at base operations around 0720 hours, Ken Yarger, Fred Adams, members of the Evaluation Team, and my boss Colonel Eldridge G. Shelton, greeted me through sleepy eyes. Colonel Shelton would co-pilot our flight that morning and, as usual, he was eager to get started.

At 0730 hours, with no indication the weather would improve, we waited for the arrival of our aircraft commander, Captain Chuck Robinson. Captain Robinson lived off base and his arrival was delayed due to the inclement weather and accidents on Highway 101. After waiting another ten minutes for Captain Robinson to arrive, and with our scheduled departure time near, Colonel Shelton arranged for a standby pilot, Lt. Colonel Ed Morrow, to pilot the aircraft. Ed Morrow arrived a short time later, and we boarded the Convair T29 twin-engine aircraft and made ready for our trip to Spokane, Washington.

Seated in my usual aisle seat facing aft with my back against a structural bulkhead, I fastened my seat belt in preparation for takeoff. Fred Adams was seated to my right, Ken Yarger was across from Fred, both men sitting next to windows.

After "Pappy", our crew chief, secured the stairwell and cabin door, Ed Morrow received taxi instructions and we sensed the cabin pressure increase. Both engines fired, the brakes released, and we began moving slowly toward our designated runway.

We taxied only a few yards before the squealing of brakes signaled we were about to stop.

"What now?" I said to Fred and Ken. "Maybe we forgot someone."

The plane stopped abruptly and rocked forward and backward several times.

"Well, might as well see what's going on," I said, and unbuckled my seat belt, grabbed the armrests and pushed myself from the seat.

Leaning forward and looking over my left shoulder into the cockpit area, I saw Pappy open the main door and lower the stairwell. The number two engine was feathered. Colonel Morrow exited the aircraft, walking smartly toward the runway apron.

"What's going on?" Fred asked.

"Robinson just showed up," I said. "Looks like we'll get underway again in a minute."

Captain Robinson, the aircraft commander came on board, buckled himself into his seat and started the number two engine, and we quickly resumed our taxi to the runway.

Reaching the departure end of the runway, the plane stopped just short of the runway and with its props turning slowly, we anticipated our clearance and final takeoff instructions.

Finally, after sitting there for a few minutes, we received our takeoff instructions and clearance from the control tower for immediate departure. The aircraft taxied to the end of the runway, engine power was advanced, and we began our takeoff roll down the runway.

Just before takeoff, Fred, Ken and I discussed the poor weather conditions and how the thick morning fog resembled large balls of cotton as it rolled in and out between pockets of clear air. We all agreed that it was not a good day to fly. As it turned out, our thoughts proved to be quite prophetic.

As the plane rose slowly from the runway, the bright morning spring sun was rising above the northeastern hills, its bright light penetrating the swirling fog. Suddenly, the white, almost incandescent, glow of the sun filled the cabin, and at last we were on our way.

After placing my briefcase under the table in front of us, I mentioned to Fred and Ken that I wanted to visit with them again about the planned inspection but first wanted to take a nap. I removed my GI-issue sunglasses, crossed my arms on the table in front of me and laid my head on my arms.

That was my last recollection of anything that was calm and ordinary.

Chapter Three: "God, don't let me die!"

"Problems are sent to us as gifts."

Anonymous

I regained consciousness, lying face down on the ground just a few yards from the burning wreckage. The top part of my body was furthermost from the fuselage. The plane was still burning and the surrounding air was heavy with the stench of burning metal, smoldering vegetation and the pungent odor of aviation fuel. It was an evil mix!

In my confusion, I imagined that what had just happened must be a nightmare, some hellish hangover, a bad dream, or a mixture of all three.

I remained on the ground for a brief moment longer trying to grasp the magnitude of what had happened, then rolled over on my back and stared at my hands. The skin on both hands hung like two softball-sized globes. Glancing at my feet, my shoes were burned and brittle, but intact, and I wondered why the lace of the left shoe was missing.

Slowly, the sensation of being on fire made me realize this was not a dream. The burning sensation on my hands, face and legs forced me to come to terms with the stark reality of my predicament. Over and over again my internal message was, "If I lie here I'm going to die, and I don't want to die. Please God, don't let me die."

My primal preservation mechanism was telling me there was little time left. I knew I had two clear choices. I could either get on my feet and walk, or remain there, get blown to hell and accept my fate !

Suddenly, through the smoke and the flames of the wreckage, cries for help from inside the shattered and burning fuselage temporarily distracted my pain, disbelief and shock. Rolling slowly over on my left side and turning clockwise on my elbows and knees, I crawled back to the burning wreckage to see if anyone else was alive. Struggling to within a few feet of the fuselage, the sounds and acrid smell of the burning airplane were punctuated with a sharp hiss followed by a muffled explosion. A blast of raw heat glanced off my face.

My first thought that no one was alive on that son-of-a-bitch proved accurate. Then faces of all the guys flashed across my mind.

Realizing I couldn't do anything to help anyone else, my instinct told me to crawl back to where I had regained consciousness, get on my feet and walk. Still on elbows and knees, I reversed course and found my movements were further restricted by pieces of the plane and eucalyptus trees shattered during the crash and impact.

In the midst of my pain and anguish I looked around a second time, hoping to see or hear other survivors. Glancing off to my right through eyes burning from the fire and smoke, I saw Bob Ward lying in a semi-fetal position about fifteen yards from me. He was charred, beginning to swell, and with small black wisps of smoke curling from his body. Then I looked to my left and saw Pappy. Pappy's head, burned almost totally black, had a small dime-sized puncture wound in the back. Blood trickled from his skull.

The magnitude of what had happened was almost impossible for me to absorb. All these good buddies wiped out at one blast and my survival was not guaranteed. Yes, survive!

"Get on your feet and walk," I screamed!

Forcing myself up on my elbows, then my knees, an excruciating pain in my lower back pulsed through my body.

"My God," I muttered, "my back must be broken."

I was determined to not let the excruciating pain stop me from walking. With a great deal of cursing and other exhortations, my mind shifted to more positive thoughts of my family and friends. Instinct told me that if my back was broken, standing would be impossible, never mind trying to walk.

Slowly, standing upright and in pain, my mind refused to grasp the destruction scattered around me on the rolling hills. What lay before me was an area of total devastation. The plane had plowed into a grove of eucalyptus trees and come to rest in an area surrounded by several small ridges to the north and east. The land sloped gently west and south away from the crash site at an angle of about thirty degrees.

The air, heavy with the smell of burning wreckage and aviation fuel, mixed with low clouds, fog and light rain, created a desolate and foreboding feeling. Was this a time warp or a lost world?

My heavy breathing and moaning for the pain to ease and for someone to help me was interrupted by my desire to see if anyone else was alive.

"Hey! Hey! Hey! Is anyone alive, is anyone alive?" I shouted, surveying the crash scene and the remains of the plane. No response.

The deathly silence was broken only by the hissing and crackling sounds of the burning plane and the strong, pungent odor of aviation fuel. The realization that my life was the only one spared began to creep into my thoughts.

All the guys were dead. Then different emotions, including fear, anxiety, anger and disbelief, began to consume me. Yet a glimmer of hope was also present in my mind. Perhaps somebody would find me. I consoled myself with the thought that a search-and-rescue mission would be initiated at the base.

"Maybe," I thought, "the team won't be able to find me and the crash site because of the rain, fog and low clouds."

As I stared into the fog and the swirling mist at the devastation around me, my spirits sank.

Gradually, the pain in my back and the burning sensation on my legs, arms, back, and face increased in intensity. Trying to decrease the awareness of pain and the accompanying anxiety, my mind again switched to more positive thoughts - my family and friends. My hopes and prayers were to see them all again. Shouting to the overcast sky, my screams continued for my wife, my children and my mother, expressing my love for them and praying to God that I would not die here like this, alone.

My only earthly companions were the fog and a constant rain falling through the swirling mist.

Standing alone and in terrible pain on that hillside, thinking about family and life, my thoughts were interrupted by the soft, wet rustling of grass and small trees. Through the mist and light fog that continued to swirl around the area, a narrow cattle trail off to my left and slightly above the crash site caught my attention. Standing in the mist and fog just beyond a clump of small trees was a small herd of white-faced cows.

The cows stopped about fifteen yards away when they saw me and appeared nervous and ready to bolt at the slightest movement. They did bolt and run when they heard me ask, "Hey, can any of you help me?"

On reflection, asking this question sounds like a silly thing to have done. However, I was desperate for anyone or anything to eliminate the pain and helplessness that was rapidly consuming me.

The stinging pain from my burns, coupled with a bone-chilling coldness began to envelop me. Shaking uncontrollably, my thoughts focused on trying to stay warm and I gently grabbed the zipper on my blue lightweight military jacket, zipping it to my neck. My left hand was totally blackened and split open from the fire. Both hands were black, and the burning pain around my neck, face and scalp felt like a million bees were stinging me.

"How long can I last?"

"Does anyone know where we are?"

"How can they find the wreckage in all this fog?"

The chilling mist engulfed me like a blanket of ice, and I felt the sands in my earthly hourglass rapidly disappearing.

Then, using some hidden unknown primal instinct, my desire to live took hold of my psyche, and I focused all my energy on walking towards a clump of waist-high grass about twenty yards away. I believed the grass would deflect some of the damp wind until someone could find me. Under the cover of a small tree in waist-high prairie grass, I curled both legs up to my chest in the fetal position and reflected on this strange irony. It was from the fetal position my life began, and it looked as if this posture would take me to the other side.

As I continued to fight the desire to sleep and tried to stay warm, my mind raced wildly over the years to my earliest childhood days.

Growing up, playing baseball and basketball, and the days of laughter with my friends and family. Treasured moments amidst my beloved parents and family.

Those memories of family and friends seemed so remote now with no chance to say good-bye. All the things which seemed important before the crash were now trivial. I realized how misplaced my priorities were as the feeling of futility swept over me. My life was slipping away and the helplessness I felt was unlike any emotion experienced before or since that day. Nothing even comes a close second.

"Please God, don't let me die," were my prayers over and over again.

Viktor Frankl, in his book *Man's Search for Meaning*, states that if a man can find a "why" to live he can endure almost any "how." Lying in that pasture, burned, cold, alone and frightened of the unknown, I was embarking on a journey which would challenge me like never before to find the "why" in my life. Finding the "how" was just the start of that journey. My feeling of being so utterly alone and helpless created the sensation that I was staring into a black hole.

Feeling drowsy and wanting to sleep, the urge to close my eyes and escape this nightmare was paramount in my mind. Sleep was too easy an option, a choice which I knew would seal my fate.

"Burk, if you fall asleep now you will never ever wake up," my inner voice screamed. "Sleep and you die, man. That's the bottom line. Think about it, for God's sake!"

Then I thought I heard voices approaching the crash site—or was my mind playing tricks on me? My instinct told me to lay perfectly still in the grass and listen with all the energy my mind could muster. Down the hill, through the fog and mist came the faint sound of voices in the distance.

Desperate for someone to find me, my strong desire to live forced me to my feet a second time, and I painfully waved my arms above my head.

"Hey! Hey! Hey! Over here! Over here!" I shouted. Then I collapsed to the ground.

Chapter Four: The Rescue

"It's not what happens to you; it's what you do about it that makes the difference."   **W Mitchell**

The voices in the pasture grew louder and a voice in the distance said, "Hey, there's a body over here in the grass." Then, as if by magic, a ruddy-faced firefighter was standing above me like an angel. He was wearing a black fire helmet and a black bunker coat with yellow reflective tape over his shoulder and across his chest. He leaned over and stared into my eyes. I was dazed, confused, and startled by his appearance. My question, "What about my face? What about my face?" was met with a cold silence.

The firefighter leaned back on his knees, paused as if to catch his breath, and shook his head slowly from side to side.

"Oh my God," he whispered, his voice breaking with emotion.

"Oh boy, Burk, you must really look like hell," I thought.

While lying in the grass before I was rescued, I noted that my scalp and head had a strange, tingly feeling. Running my right hand through my hair revealed that my hair and scalp were white ash lying lifeless on the palm of my hand and powdering down over my face.

The firefighters placed me gently on white Vaseline-covered sheets, lifted me onto a gurney and carried me to a waiting Coast Guard helicopter for the flight back to the base hospital. As the gurney was lifted through the open door of the helicopter, I was met by an Air Force Staff Sergeant, a member of the base Search and Rescue Team. He began asking me about my family, the accident, and other questions framed to maintain my connection to reality. After responding to his questions, I asked if he knew a specific Master Sergeant. "Yes, I do Captain," he replied, "We play squash and run together almost every day."

"Tell him hello," I said.

"You bet I will," he replied.

The incessant chatter with my rescuers was another desperate attempt to distract myself from the painful reality of the crash. Remembering all this years later, I can't help but chuckle over the interactions with the people who saved my life. The feeble attempt to stay matter-of-fact seems so silly now, but maybe it was really important at the time to shield my mind from the overwhelming reality that my body was suffering.

While in the helicopter, my thoughts about the crash and what would happen to me and my family were interrupted by a stinging sensation on my upper right arm and the drug-induced sleep that followed was a welcome relief.

Some time later, my senses were revived by the total chaos and bedlam of the emergency room as doctors, nurses and corpsmen worked feverishly on my injuries. Curiously, I was probably the calmest person in the room, but perhaps this was simply due to the shot administered earlier by the corpsmen.

Lying on the gurney and looking up at the nurses and doctors standing nearby, I asked one of the nurses what they were doing to me. Feeling the lower part of my right pant leg move and glancing at my feet, I saw a nurse cut away the lower part of my trouser leg and remove my shoe and sock. Then I felt a sharp sting on the lower part of my right leg. As the doctors and nurses continued shouting instructions to one another, a nurse kneeled near my head and whispered in my right ear that all would be well. She told me the sting was an intravenous needle inserted into my leg.

Two corpsmen then turned the gurney around, rolled it to the elevator and escorted me downstairs to have my back and spine X-rayed. An Air Force doctor, walking beside me, leaned over and whispered in my ear, "Hang in there, Captain. We need to take X-rays to see how badly your back is injured."

I was concerned about a possible additional effect of X-rays increasing the severity of my burns. The post-crash fire had burned away nearly all the skin on my legs, back, arms and face, leaving my body one large open wound. The hospital staff at the base were not trained to handle burns of this magnitude but they did all they could to make me as comfortable as possible.

When the X-rays were completed, the corpsmen returned me to the emergency room and positioned the gurney near the rear exit door.

Lying there waiting to be taken to the flight-line, familiar voices behind and to my left temporarily distracted me.

As I lifted my head and peered over my left shoulder, I saw my wife and my boss, Colonel Joe Johnson, standing nearby.

"I'm sorry," I whispered through a swollen and blackened face.

My guilt and confusion as the sole survivor of the crash and my deteriorating mental state made me feel as if I had to apologize that the crash had occurred and that I was unable to save the others.

My thoughts about family and retracing the crash over and over again were interrupted by a loud bang on the emergency exit door. The door flew open and the gurney, with a corpsmen at each end, was lifted into the back of a blue Air Force ambulance for the short drive to the flight line. With all the commotion around me, I continued to struggle with understanding what had happened to me and talked incessantly to the Air Force doctor crouched next to the gurney. I recounted the crash sequence endlesslessly and continued to fret over my inability to save the others. I continued to question where I was and where all this was going, and I asked the doctor over and over again to notify my family and ensure they were okay. The doctor assured me everything would be all right and my family was fine.

"We're here at the flight line," he said. "The plane just landed and we'll get you on board as fast as we can."

The ambulance stopped and the two corpsmen sitting in the front seat got out, walked to the rear of the ambulance and opened both doors to a gray haze-overcast sky and light rain.

In the distance, the whine of jet engines and the aroma of jet fuel hung so heavily in the air it was like I could taste it. This thought temporarily distracted me from the pain.

"Hey, that sounds like a C-141," I thought.

"A C-141 has landed and is taking you to the burn unit at Fort Sam Houston in San Antonio," the doctor said, again interrupting my meandering thoughts.

I didn't know anything about the burn unit at Fort Sam Houston, but I was about to become very intimately aware of it.

At that moment, deep inside, I couldn't pretend to myself that this was not real, even though I wished and prayed to awaken and be freed from this enormously horrible dream.

I pleaded with God to let me live, though I wasn't really sure exactly what that meant at this time.

Sole survivor of Air Force plane crash here recalls May tragedy

Futher details on the recovery of Captain George A. Burk, sole survivor of the May 4, 1970 Air Force plane crash on the Mangels ranch south of Sonoma, were revealed in an article appearing in last week's issue of The Sonoma Index-Tribune.

As The Sonoma Index-Tribune story of Jan. 28 stated, the 29-year-old Air Force communications officer is on convalescent leave with his family from Brooke Army Medical Center's Institute of Surgical Research, Ft. Houston, Texas awaiting reconstructive surgery on his hand.

Captain Burk was flown to the famed Army burn center critically injured with second and third degree burns over 60 per cent of the body surface.

The Air Force communications officer's wife and three children live in family quarters at Fort Sam Houston. He has been with his family most of the time since last October while he has continued his hospital treatment as an outpatient. He is expected to have his hand surgery in about two weeks.

CAPTAIN BURK says that he feels very good and that he has regained most of the weight lost immediately after his injury. He is now able to drive his car.

A veteran of six and a half years with the Air Force, Captain Burk was assigned to the Western Communications Regional Headquarters at Hamilton Air Force Base.

Captain Burk recalled many of the details of the crash which took the lives of four crew members and nine passengers, most of them communications specialists and many of them close personal friends.

The plane, a T-29 transport, left Hamilton Air Force Base at 8 a.m. May 4 for a flight to Fairchild Air Force Base, near Spokane, Wash. After a normal take-off the plane climbed to an altitude of about 5,000 feet when trouble developed. The air craft began to vibrate violently and all aboard were advised to take standard crash positions.

He recalls that the plane began to dive at about a 20 degree altitude. He remembers preparing for the crash but he does not recall any of the details when the plane hit a fog-shrouded knoll on the Mangels ranch.

NEXT THING he remembers about 25 yards from the burning wreckage. John Davieau, resident manager of the ranch here, was the first to reach the crash scene and to smothered Captain Burk's burning clothes.

Capt. Burk remembers the rescue helicopters coming to the scene from Hamilton. He waved his arm and the rescue crews immediately found him and flew him back to the base hospital.

Medical officers there immediately contacted the Institute of Surgical Research and a burn team flew to the west coast base and returned the badly burned officer to Brooke the same day.

Captain Burk is looking forward, after further hospitalization, to returning to duty as a communications officer. Meanwhile, he, his wife, and their children — Walter J, Kimberly Ann, and Scott E, will reside at Fort Sam Houston.

OF THE fatal motor-vehicle accidents in the United States during 1969, reports the National Automobile Club, 2,200 were both in collisions.

Lone survivor recalls dive, recovers at BAMC

The sole survivor of an Air Force plane crash in California on May 4, 1970, has recovered from his burn injuries at Brooke Army Medical Center's Institute of Surgical Research and is on convalescent leave with his family awaiting reconstructive surgery on his hand.

Captain George A. Burk was flown to the famed Army burn center critically injured with second and third degree burns over 60 per cent of his body surface.

The Air Force communications officer's wife and three children live in family quarters at Ft. Sam Houston. He has been with his family most of the time since last October while he has continued his hospital treatment as an outpatient. He is expected to have his hand surgery in about two weeks.

CPT Burk says that he feels very good and that he has regained most of the weight lost immediately after his injury. He is now able to drive his car.

A veteran of six and a half years with the Air Force, CPT Burk was assigned to the Western Communications Regional Headquarters at Hamilton Air Force Base, Calif.

CPT Burk recalled many of the details of the crash which took the lives of four crew members and nine passengers, most of them communications specialists and many of them close personal friends. The plane, a T-29 transport, left Hamilton AFB at 8 a.m. on May 4 for a flight to Fairchild Air Force Base, near Spokane, Wash. After a normal take-off the plane climbed to an altitude of about 5,000 feet when trouble developed. The aircraft began to vibrate violently and all aboard were advised to take standard crash positions. He recalls that the plane began to dive at about a 20 degree altitude. He remembers preparing for the crash but he does not recall any of the details when the plane hit a fog-shrouded hill top.

Next thing he remembers was regaining consciousness about 25 yards from the burning wreckage. A rancher living in the area was the first to reach the crash scene, and he extinguished CPT Burk's burning clothes. He remembers the rescue helicopters coming to the scene from Hamilton AFB. He waved his arm and the rescue crews immediately found him and flew him back to the base hospital at Hamilton. Medical officers there immediately contacted the Institute of Surgical Research and a burn team flew to the west coast base and returned the badly burned officer to Brooke the same day.

CPT Burk is looking forward, after further hospitalization, to returning to duty as a communications officer. Meanwhile, he, his wife, and their children — Walter J., Kimberly Ann, and Scott E, will reside at FSH.

Local air crash survivor

Capt. George A. Burk, sole survivor of a plane crash on the Mangels ranch, south of Sonoma, last May, leaves Brooke Army Medical Center's famed Institute of Surgical Research after recovering from critical burns.
—(Army Photo).

Lone survivor of Sonoma air crash has recovered

HAMILTON AFB -- The sole survivor of the May 4 air crash that claimed 13 lives on the Mangels ranch, south of Sonoma, has recovered from burns that covered more than 60 per cent of his body, according to the public information office at Hamilton Air Force Base.

Captain George Burk, 29, survived the crash of the Air Force transport plane, which plowed into the rolling hills here shortly after takeoff from Hamilton. Captain Burk's calls for help were heard by Mangels ranch manager John Davieau who arrived on the scene shortly after the tragedy. Davieau's prompt emergency aid is credited with helping to save Captain Burk's life.

The communications officer is presently in Texas on convalescent leave from Brooke Army Medical Center at Ft. Houston, Texas.

Articles from the *Sonoma Index-Tribune*, January 28, 1971

Where 13 died in flaming crash

An Air Force T-29 transport crashed early Monday morning on the Mangels ranch in Schellville soon after its takeoff from Hamilton Air Force Base. Thirteen of the 14 servicemen aboard were killed as the big plane slammed into a tree-dotted knoll three miles west of Arnold drive in the bleak, fog-shrouded hills. At upper left, a Coast Guard helicopter is about to land to receive the one survivor, Capt. George A. Burk, who is in critical condition. In photo can be seen, just below the chopper, Allan Norrbom's ambulance and near the trees Norrbom and other rescuers with Burk strapped to a gurney. At upper right is a wheel and a portion of the fuselage. Lower left, California Highway Patrolmen, Hamilton AFB servicemen and ranchers search the burning wreckage for bodies. All 13 of the dead were accounted for and later identified at Travis AFB. Below, right, is one of the biggest pieces of wreckage, one of the plane's two motors. Fragments of the plane littered an area of a couple of acres. Air Force investigators are still at the crash site, continuing probe for cause of crash.

Pictures from the *Sonoma Index-Tribune* the day after the crash.

Chapter Five: A Time Of Reflection

"As our case is new, we must think and act anew."
Abraham Lincoln

While on the gurney in the back of the Air Force ambulance, many of the events in my life played over and over in my mind. Several of them, sources of irritation before, now seemed irrelevant and meaningless. I still couldn't quite grasp what was happening. I think the doctor sensed my frustration and fear so he crouched next to me and talked to me in reassuring tones.

Hundreds of memories rushed through my mind—about home, childhood, playing ball, college days, my wife and children, and my deepest wish to turn back and not have this happen. I prayed for forgiveness and for God to grant me another chance at life.

I'd often heard the old adage that there are no atheists in foxholes or bunkers. I found that was true in Vietnam, and I found faith driven home again as I lay burned and broken outside a burning plane on a hillside in Northern California.

The whine of the jet engines stopped and voices, faint at first, grew louder as they approached the ambulance.

Slowly lifting my head and peering over the tops of my feet, I saw two men wearing white hospital uniforms approaching the open doors.

"Must be two corpsmen from the burn unit," I thought.

The pain from the burns and pain in my lower back, chest, neck, face and shoulders, forced me to lower my head on the pillow. Then I saw a person standing next to the gurney whose uniform was a different shade of tan than my summer weight khaki uniform.

"It's an Army uniform, must be from Fort Sam Houston and the burn unit," I thought.

After he introduced himself to me and the Air Force doctor, they began discussing the crash and my injuries.

The Air Force doctor seemed preoccupied with my lower back and spinal injuries and offered advice about my treatment. Unknown to me at the time, the Army physician was a doctor from the burn unit.

The two doctors continued a lengthy dialogue about my injuries and the planned medical treatment. All the while, my exasperation, impatience, and nervousness continued to increase.

Finally, my exasperation got the best of me.

"Hey, will you guys stop arguing and get me on that damn airplane," I said, interrupting their conversation. Suddenly aware that I was listening, they responded, "Oh . . . yeah . . . right."

The two corpsmen standing nearby grabbed the gurney, one at each end, and carried me across the tarmac, up the rear exit ramp into the plane and lifted me onto a stretcher attached to the right side of the aircraft bulkhead.

Lying on the gurney, feeling groggy, uncomfortable, scared, and still trying to grasp what happened, a movement to my right caught my attention. As my eyes focused, I could make out a woman dressed in her summer weight blue uniform standing next to me. What a pleasant sight for my burned eyes. An attractive blonde Air Force flight nurse smiling at me like an angel. My reaction provided a glimpse of normalcy that helped reduce some of my anxiety.

"Wow! She came over here to talk to me," I thought.

"Are you thirsty, Captain?" she asked in a quiet and reassuring tone.

"Yes," I murmured.

The nurse disappeared and returned a few seconds later with an ice chip.

"Captain, open your mouth," she said and placed an ice chip on my tongue.

"An ice chip?!" I yelled. "What the hell is going on?"

"We must measure all of your fluid intake," she said.

"Damn it, I'm lying here dying of thirst and she gives me one ice chip," I thought.

The feelings of thirst added to my frustration and anxiety. It now seems incredible that something as simple as thirst could be so intense and overwhelming. I was obsessed and it was as intense as any emotion I had ever experienced in my life.

I was insane with thirst!

"Please God, don't let me die," I pleaded.

My pleas for survival were meshed with sobs, then sleep was again a welcome respite.

Suddenly, I was jolted awake by the screeching of tires and reverse thrust of engines. The C-141 Starlifter changed directions, and the whine of the engines indicated we landed and were taxiing.

"Where are we?" I groggily asked the nurse.

"Kelly Air Force Base," she said. "You'll be airlifted to the hospital from here."

After the plane came to a complete stop and its engines were silent, its rear doors opened to a bright, sunny, humid, Texas afternoon. Two corpsmen approached my stretcher, removed the straps holding the gurney to the side of the plane's fuselage and carried me down the ramp and out the rear exit of the plane. In the distance, the whine of a helicopter engine and the "whup, whup,

whup" of its rotor blades slowly whirling and increasing in speed cut through the hot Texas afternoon. Still in a semi-conscious state, I couldn't believe that this was real. Even with the vivid sensation of hot air blowing in and around the open helicopter, the bumping and sliding as the corpsmen slid the gurney into the helicopter, my mind was still looking for a way to believe the dream would end.

"I don't want to die," I thought over and over again.

Then sleep once again engulfed me like a warm blanket on a cold afternoon.

My sleep was interrupted a second time by the sound of a loud bang, followed by a second and third noise. I opened my eyes and discovered I was lying on a mobile cart in an elevator with several corpsmen and a nurse dressed in white medical uniforms standing near me. The only noise was the soft whine of the elevator and the whirl of its exhaust fan. With my mind still operating in fast forward, I wondered why someone was playing this nasty trick on me.

"Boy, will I get even with them," I thought.

Closing my eyes, my prayers continued that I wouldn't die and that the constant pain and discomfort would go away.

Chapter Six: This Is Going To Sting

"Don't just do something, lay there."　　　　**Anonymous**

The elevator door slowly opened. The corpsmen and nurse guided the cart to the right, then to the left. I heard a loud "boom" as we raced through a set of double doors and down the hallway. We turned abruptly left again, and I heard another "boom" as we entered through a second door. Then all movement stopped and for a brief few seconds, all was quiet except for my moaning and squirming in pain.

When I opened my eyes, I was overwhelmed by the glare of several large lights that engulfed my face. Working feverishly around the table were nurses, corpsmen and a doctor. Their bodies and movements were partially obscured and filmy because of my facial swelling and the bright lights blurring my vision.

"I'm going to clean your burns with Phisohex and it's going to sting," a female nurse said.

"No shit!" I yelled as she began washing my face and arms.

"When were you born?" a second nurse asked.

"July 9, 1941."

"Where were you born?" she asked again.

"Pittsburgh, Pennsylvania."

"Are you married?"

"Yes."

"What's your wife's name?"

"Nancy," I responded.

"Do you have children?"

"Yes."

"What are their names?"

"Walter, Kimberly and Scott. Please make this all go away," I pleaded. "I don't want to die!"

"Are you allergic to anything?" she asked.

"Yes!" I yelled, pausing to catch my breath and trying to handle my discomfort.

Suddenly, everything was still as the staff stopped working to listen to my reply. The room was eerily quiet.

"Fire!" I yelled.

While the nurses continued to clean my wounds and a corpsmen cut off my uniform and removed my shoes, I felt like all that was left of my life was zipping past me like a speeding freight train. I again was mercifully rescued from the pain in my back and from the burns over my whole body as I passed out. I awoke lying in a bed in the Intensive Care Unit (ICU).

My skin itched and burned simultaneously, and my desire for water was all-consuming. Tubes trailed from my nose and penis to disappear into bottles above my head and into unseen containers hidden someplace underneath my bed. My arms and legs, elevated and wrapped in heavy, white gauze dressings, were attached to metal chains suspended from the top frame of the bed. As some small concession to modesty, a small, white cloth covered my genital area.

Even in a burn unit, there is some privacy.

"Whadda ya know," I recall thinking. "Just like Adam, I'm wearing a fig leaf."

A color television set was positioned to my right, permitting me to watch a baseball game between the St. Louis Cardinals and the Atlanta Braves. Trying to keep track of the game was challenging and extremely frustrating. My short-term memory had deteriorated, and every event allowed only a brief glimpse as it flew by and disappeared, to be swallowed up someplace in the pain and distress.

Failure to remember simple things like the batter, score and inning increased my frustration, anxiety and sense of physical disarray. With each passing minute, my patience grew shorter and my anger more intense.

The staff was forever trying to reinforce my connection to reality by asking my name, where I was born, childrens' and parents' names and other details of my background. I struggled with frustration over the difficulty in recalling these ordinary bits of information.

My emotions were further compounded because of my inability to recall the precise time of day and the day of the week when the crash occurred and if, in fact, the plane had crashed. My only relief from this nightmare was to close my eyes and hope this was all just a bad dream.

"When I wake up, my family will be here and tell me this is all a bad dream," I kept repeating.

Wrapped like a mummy and lying in an Army Hospital, burned, and every cell in my body screaming for water, my mind kept trying to tell me this was all a dream.

"Damn it, this must be a dream," I yelled to myself.

"What have I done to deserve this? Am I really that terrible a person to deserve this kind of punishment?" I asked.

"My body feels like I'm on fire, and I itch at the same time. My back hurts like hell. Am I going to die like this? Mom! Please make all this go away," I begged.

"Please God, don't let me die," I prayed.

At a time like this, it was funny how my thoughts went back to an earlier time and the protection of my mother.

Even as I thought about her, I heard a familiar voice, and straining to see out of the corner of my right eye, I saw, standing next to the bed, my mother.

"Oh, Mom!" I blurted and started to cry.

Then I closed my eyes and escaped back into unconsciousness.

Chapter Seven: Interrogation in the ICU

"The way we communicate is the problem."
Stephen Covey

In the Intensive Care Unit, time became harder and harder to measure. Seconds seemed like minutes, minutes like hours, and hours seemed like days. I literally lost touch with any sense of time and the reality of my life. All my energy was focused on fighting for every breath and trying to deal with the pain.

It was, I believe, a few days later when in a morphine induced stupor, I heard voices around my bed and opened my eyes.

"Hi Doc," I said. "What are you doing?"

"You can't feel that, George?" he asked

"Feel what, Doc?" I asked.

The "what" he was doing was cutting open my right leg from above the ankle to below my knee and removing an infected vein. The infection was the result of dirt entering my blood stream on the tip of the needle inserted into my right ankle in the emergency room at Hamilton AFB.

After the vein was removed, Dr. Inge left the ICU and returned a short time later. Standing at the foot of my bed, he appeared to be doing something with my feet and toes.

"Can you feel this?" he asked.

"Feel what, Doc?" I replied.

"This," he said.

"I don't know what you're doing, Doc," I slurred, "but I don't feel a thing."

Dr. Inge was poking needles into the soles of my feet and my toes, trying to determine if I was paralyzed. Even though I had no feeling in my legs or feet, it was apparent he wanted a response to his intense questioning.

"Up or down?" Dr. Inge asked.

"Up," I muttered.

"Up or down?" he asked repeatedly.

"Up," I muttered again.

"Down," I muttered a third time.

Although testing my muscular responses probably only lasted only a few minutes, it seemed much longer! What they surmised was true. I had no feeling in my feet, nor could I determine if the pins were placed on the heels of my feet or my toes. However, to help pass the time and alleviate my boredom, I decided to turn the experiment into a game. Hey, why not? What did I have to lose?

Morphine continued to cloud my mental acuity, and it was difficult to distinguish between reality and dreams of torture.

One day I am sure of, I opened my eyes and saw Dr. Inge standing at the right side of my bed, dressed in his usual apparel—bonnet, mask, gloves and surgical gown.

"George," he said. "You have some visitors. Two men want to talk to you about the crash."

"Aw, f_ _ _!" I muttered. "I don't want to talk to anyone now. Why don't they leave me alone."

Off to my right and walking behind Dr. Inge were two men dressed in bonnets, masks, gloves and gowns. One man carried what appeared to be a small tape recorder.

"Oh no," I thought. "Two more gawkers. Just what I need."

The man carrying the tape recorder walked around the foot of the bed and placed the recorder on the small green table to my left; the second man stood to my right. With a click of a button, the interview started.

"This is going to be an interrogation, not an interview," I thought.

The physical distress from the burns, coupled with the excruciating pain in my back, chest, shoulders and neck, created the feeling that my body was a large exposed nerve. All my nonverbal senses were elevated, making me acutely aware of the visitors' uneasiness.

That evened the playing field a bit. They didn't want to be there talking with me and the feeling was mutual.

"Tell us what happened, Captain Burk," he asked.

I began to recite precisely what happened the day of the crash. From the crack appearing in the window to the rapid decompression, my standing up after the impact, then everything going blank.

"After the plane stopped moving," I continued, my mind in fast forward, "I unbuckled my seat belt, stood up, turned towards the aisle, felt a lot of heat, then everything went black. I dug my way out through a crack in the fuselage."

"That's impossible, Captain," he replied. "You were found forty yards from the crash site. With your internal injuries, you couldn't have dug your way out!"

Knowing they didn't believe me made me mad as hell. I became even more animated, started to shake uncontrollably and began swearing at them.

"Get out of here. You're killing my patient," I heard Dr. Inge demand.

The interviewers left the ICU without securing my statement about the crash.

Three days later, another interview was conducted by the same two individuals with the same results.

Once again, when I recounted that I dug my way out of the crash, the lead interviewer again questioned the accuracy of my recollection. His challenging the veracity of my statement made me more animated. I started swearing at them again and shook more violently.

"You're killing my patient. Get out of here," Dr. Inge demanded the second time.

As a result of their stubborn disbelief of my recollection, the investigation team never did receive my statement to put in the accident report. All they needed to do was turn on the recorder, ask me one question, be quiet, and they would have gotten a full account. I still wonder why people have to make life difficult for themselves like that.

Approximately six months later, Dr. Inge told me the investigation team was unable to pinpoint the cause of the crash and were prepared to attribute it to pilot error, bird strike, or "cause of accident-unknown".

All that remained of that twin-engine Convair T-29 aircraft was the vertical stabilizer (the tail section) and one of the two engines.

Nine months after the crash, when it was clear I would live, my family told me about their first meeting with Dr. Inge. That first meeting occurred in the early morning hours of May 5th in the small waiting area just outside the main ward, Ward 14A.

Like most people, they had no experience with someone who had severe burns. Not understanding the pervasive effect of burn injuries, my family's initial concern was mainly for my broken back and internal injuries. They were unprepared for Dr. Inge's response. Dr. Inge stated there was little he could do for me except make me as comfortable as possible.

He described the enhanced susceptibility to viruses and bacterial diseases as well as other medical complications that follow a massive disruption of the skin's defenses. Typically, the burn survivor's situation deteriorates from these secondary effects for the first fourteen days after the injury. The only reason he expected me to live up to fourteen days was my excellent physical condition.

As a physically fit non-smoker, I had stored protein and muscle tissue that my body could survive on for a short period of time, but after that, the prognosis was discouraging.

"What you are telling us, Doctor, is that he is unlikely to make it past the first fourteen days?" my wife asked, dumbfounded.

"That's correct," he replied. "I'm afraid that's the situation."

My wife and my mother were in total shock. They both felt like someone had just punched them in the stomach.

Meanwhile, with each passing hour in the ICU, my responses to external verbal and physical stimuli from my family, the doctors, nurses and corpsmen became less pronounced. My breathing became more labored, the pain was increasing, and my grasp of reality was slowly ebbing away. My subconscious mind was preparing me to die. However, my strong male ego was still intact.

While in the ICU, I opened my eyes at the sudden movement near my bed. What I saw was Mrs. Collins, one of the civilian ICU nurses, gently tucking in the sheets and talking to me in a soft, reassuring voice.

"George," she said, "we're trying to keep you warm."

Then she continued to "stroke my mind" by telling me what she was going to do, why she was doing it, and that everything would be all right. It was, "George this" and "George that," over and over again.

A one-sided conversation which lasted I guess, for several minutes.

"I'm a Captain in the United States Air Force and don't you ever forget it!" I blurted out, exasperated she woke me up and was bothering me.

Obviously, I didn't see or hear her reaction, but months later, when Sheri McGhee mentioned the episode to me, the incident came flooding back from deep inside my sub-conscious mind.

"Do you remember saying that to her, Captain Burk?" Sheri asked.

"Kinda," I said. "I vaguely remember her talking to me. The sound of her voice really irritated me, and I didn't want to be bothered."

"Well," Sheri said, "we all had a laugh at that one. It was obvious to us your ego was still working."

"You know what else she did?" Sheri asked.

Nope," I replied, "but I bet you're gonna tell me."

"Right after that happened, Mrs. Collins contacted Dr. Inge and told him about your response. Dr. Inge then told everyone from then on to call you 'Captain Burk,' " she continued.

"In fact," she said, "let me show you something," and walked behind the nurses' station and grabbed my medical records.

"See," she said, opening my medical records, "There's the note in your medical records instructing everyone to call you 'Captain Burk'. "

Mrs. Collins could have dismissed my comment as irrational blather and gone about her work. However, she made a conscious choice to tell Dr. Inge in the hope that something positive, however remote, could result from my comment.

While talking to Sheri about this incident, I suddenly became aware that, while I was still in the ICU, in bed on the wards or on a gurney returning from the operating room, doctors, nurses, and even the maintenance staff and secretaries always greeted me in the same way.

"Hello, Captain Burk, how are you doing?" they would ask.

This is another example of the professionalism and caring the people at the burn unit showed to me and my family.

As a team dedicated to my recovery, they were determined not to let any stone go unturned if the stone would give me an extra chance to live.

Chapter Eight: The Bridge Never Crossed

It was during my three-month stay in the ICU when my two near-death experiences (NDE's) occurred.

In July, 1970, during one of Dr. Inge's daily visits with my family, he discussed my status and his short-term prognosis.

"I'm afraid George is giving up. There is nothing more we can do for him except to keep him as comfortable as possible," he said.

He told them my heart beat was once every ten seconds, the pupils of my eyes had dilated, my breathing was more shallow and labored, and I was expected to die within a few hours.

While in the ICU, my family was notified on ten separate occasions that my death was a matter of days or even hours away. During a call to my Uncle Hardie Beck in Pittsburgh, my mother told him to arrange the handling of my body with a local funeral home as my death was expected in a few hours. Nancy and my mother agreed I would be buried next to my Uncle Howard (Dutch) Beck and my mother's parents.

What my family and the medical staff did not know was that during this time my soul was experiencing something so wonderful and unbelievable, no one who has not been there could understand.

My first near-death experience began with a vision of visiting Colonel Shelton. Suddenly, I discovered myself walking side-by-side with him on the deck of a three-level cruise liner. Colonel Shelton was wearing his orange flight suit and I wore my khaki summer weight uniform. Neither of us displayed any external burn injuries, and he was walking without difficulty.

The cruise ship had three rails with support poles approximately every five feet apart, and the floor was shiny teakwood. Each side of the deck had three doors which opened to a large, well-lighted room.

With his left arm wrapped securely around my right arm and helping me walk, we entered the room through a middle door. Standing three deep around an oval shaped bar awaiting service were people of all ages, sizes and gender; they were all smiling and appeared to be enjoying themselves.

As we approached the bar, my confusion over what I was seeing increased.

"C'mon George, I'll buy you a drink," Colonel Shelton said.

"No thanks, Colonel, I'm too sick to drink. I have to sit down," I replied.

I glanced around the room for a place to sit and noticed a small booth along a wall to my left. Seated in the booth were two older couples. The construction resembled an old soda fountain booth with seats covered in red vinyl; the table was oval-shaped with an aluminum strip around its edge.

Then, as if by magic, I found myself seated between the two couples at the table. All the while, the disturbance in my stomach continued to increase and my body became colder.

"Something strange is happening here," I thought, "but what?"

Not knowing what was happening scared me. I noted that, sitting in this large room with all these people, all I could hear was my breathing, but not the voices from the other guests. Looking at the couple to my left, then the couple to my right, I realized their mouths were moving but there wasn't any sound that I could hear.

Then it dawned on me.

"These people are all dead. If they are not dead, why couldn't I hear them?" I thought.

The scene really puzzled me and I wondered what was going to happen. Then, fifteen or thirty minutes later (I still don't know why those numbers are important), Colonel Shelton walked over to me.

"C'mon George, it's time to go, " he said, looking down at me.

"I don't want to go with you, Colonel. I'm too young to die. I have too much to live for."

Without disturbing the others at the table, Colonel Shelton lifted me up and over the table and placed his left arm through my right arm. Then, arm in arm, we walked out of the room onto the deck through two swinging wooden doors. The sickness in my stomach and the cold feeling continued to increase. After we walked through the two swinging doors, we turned right and walked towards a wooden enclosed bridge. All the while I watched the other passengers walk past us towards the bridge. Throughout this process, the only person communicating with me was Colonel Shelton. As we approached the wooden enclosed bridge, it became more difficult for me to breathe.

We walked the thirty feet or so to where the bridge was attached to the boat's deck. Unable to lift my legs, we stopped so I could grasp each leg behind the knee and lift my legs to the bridge. We then continued our journey to the other side.

The faces on all the other passengers are still a vivid memory to me. They were happy and of all ages, men and women. As we continued across the bridge, the feeling of cold and sickness continued to engulf me until I had to shuffle my feet across the bridge's flooring.

Reaching the mid-point of our journey, I wanted to pause and consider where we were headed.

"We're half-way to where we're going," I thought. "I've got to use the last bit of my strength to break free from his grasp and go back to the boat. I'm too young to die and have too much to live for."

Then with a grunt, I pulled my right arm free from his left arm, turned to my left, looked up and saw a bright light, a door and smelled the strong scent of flowers. I knew it was the other side.

I continued to turn slowly to my left and shuffled back to the boat. Colonel Shelton made no attempt to stop me. As I approached the boat's deck, the sick feeling and cold began to dissipate. When I finally reached the deck, I turned to my right and looked back into the bridge. There was Colonel Shelton, tall, ramrod straight and in his orange flight suit, walking through the door and into a bright light. The sweet, pungent scent of flowers rafted throughout the bridge. My near-death experience ended as rapidly as it began.

My wife, my mother and several nurses were standing around my bed. My eyes opened and my voice startled them.

"The light! The light!" I yelled.

"What light, George? What light?" they asked.

"The light! The light!" I yelled, my voice rising in pitch.

Believing the glare from the lights surrounding my bed was too bright for my eyes, the nurses rearranged the lights. Everyone was confused and shaken by my apparent incoherence.

After several minutes of screaming about the light, my shaking increased and my voice continued to rise. The nurses increased the dosage of morphine forcing me into a another drug-induced sleep.

My second near-death experience occurred while I was in a coma.

Suddenly, I found myself looking down a long, narrow tunnel into a bright light. Standing in front of the bright light were two shadows. Then in a loud 'whoosh,' Fred Adams and Kenny Yarger were standing in front of me.

"Fred, Ken, what the hell are you guys doing here?" I asked.

"It's all right, Captain Burk. We're okay, but you need to get better," Fred replied in his slow, lisped speech. Then with a second loud 'whoosh,' Fred and Ken disappeared down the tunnel as quickly as they appeared.

Understanding these visions became important, and I sought help from the person I most trusted to know what I was going through. That person was Dr. Inge.

In late October 1970, five months after the crash, I had my first discussion about the visions with Dr. Inge. I felt that if I shared my experiences with him he could help me interpret them. I was not disappointed!

After I described my two experiences in detail, Dr. Inge crossed his arms on his chest, glanced at the ceiling and, looking like he had not heard anything unusual, he said, "George, what you have experienced is what we call the will to survive. I think everyone who dies experiences what you did."

"Well, Doc, " I asked. "What do you believe in?"

At first, Dr. Inge appeared puzzled by my question. "What do you mean 'believe in,' George?" he asked.

"What do you believe in Doc?" I asked a second time.

"Well, George," he said. "If you mean do I believe in God, I believe that every time I'm performing surgery in the operating room, God is whispering in my ear and telling me what to do."

For a brief moment, the room was still as we both just stared at each other. Then, I removed the pillows from under my buttocks and legs and prepared to leave.

"Where are you going?" he asked, startled by my abrupt movement.

"Well, Doc," I said, "If that's what you believe, that's good enough for me. I'm tired and gonna go back downstairs and take a nap."

That morning, as I shuffled out of the room, I started to understand what had happened to me, and I began to feel as if there were some meaning to what I had been going through.

Over the next few months, visits with Dr. Inge, the nurses and corpsmen were more frequent. I had known most of them only as voices and hands while in the ICU, so I felt as if I were getting to know them as people for the first time. So many questions remained and too few answers.

My conversations with Dr. Inge and the hospital staff helped me learn who was involved in my rescue and recovery so that I could reconstruct the missing time during my three month stay in the ICU.

Up to this point, approximately six months after the crash, only Dr. Inge and my family knew who the rancher was who had extinguished the fire on my body and made the first critical difference leading to my survival.

His discovery of me was accidental and followed an unlikely chain of events that reinforces my belief in God, miracles, and that we all have angels who subtly affect the flow of our destiny.

Chapter Nine: Letter to Mom

"If you don't do something differently, you'll end up where you are headed." **Gary Koyen**

By October 1970, my parents' life at home in Pittsburgh had finally returned to a level of normalcy as they anxiously awaited my visit during the Christmas holidays. One early Saturday morning my mother, sitting at the dining room table enjoying a cup of coffee, started opening the previous day's mail.

Sifting through stacks of bills, advertisements and letters, a letter with a California address caught her eye. The address piqued her attention. Mom was totally unprepared for the letter's contents.

The letter was from Mrs. Pearl Davieau of Schellville, California. The contents of Pearl's letter left my mother speechless and dumbfounded.

After briefly introducing herself and her family, Pearl began weaving a tale my mother found difficult to believe. She and her husband, John Davieau, had managed a two-thousand acre cattle ranch near Schellville, California, for the previous twenty-five years. Schellville is a few miles southwest of Napa.

As part of his Monday morning routine, John would climb into his four-wheel drive pick-up truck and drive around the ranch in search of dead, injured or stray cattle. The terrain on the ranch was hilly, with numerous ravines and washes.

On this particular Monday morning, May 4, 1970, John surveyed the area for an hour. Realizing the fog, low clouds and light rain restricted his ability to see any dead or stray cattle, he decided to return to the farmhouse. Driving the few remaining yards to the northeast gate, he stopped and reversed course. With the windows in the truck rolled down, he descended slowly down a craggy, rock-strewn ravine, a ravine which he had never driven through in his previous twenty-five years on the ranch.

"What are the neighbors doing burning on a day like today?" he thought, as he reached the bottom of the ravine and smelled smoke. He turned the truck towards the smoke to investigate its source. As the truck lurched slowly over the rocks and furrows up the opposite side of the ravine, John was totally unprepared for what he was about to see. As the front of the truck slowly topped the ravine, his thoughts remained focused on why the neighbors were burning debris when the weather was so bad. Gazing through the front window, he thought his eyes were playing tricks on him. There, in the pasture about fifty yards away, was an airplane that had crashed and was burning.

John Davieu

"I'd better see if anyone is still alive," he exclaimed and depressed the accelerator pedal to the floor.

Racing towards the burning wreckage as fast as he could, the hilly and rock-strewn terrain bounced John around in the truck's cab like a rag doll. Reaching the crash scene, he slammed on the brakes, jumped out of the truck and found me on fire amidst the intense heat of the burning wreckage.

"John threw dirt all over your son to put out the fire on his body, then jumped back in his truck and drove as fast as he could here to the farmhouse," Pearl continued in her letter.

Arriving at the farmhouse out of breath, he excitedly told Pearl about the crash and called Hamilton Air Force Base.

"Are you people missing a plane?" he asked the person who answered his call.

"Yes," was the reply.

"Well, I just found one on fire in my field," he replied.

After providing a general location of the crash scene to the base emergency dispatcher, John raced out the farmhouse, jumped back into his truck and began the bumpy drive back to the crash scene. When he returned, he saw the first group of rescuers extinguishing the fires and removing the few bodies that remained. It was a ghastly scene.

It wasn't until many months later, in October, 1970, that I learned of the circumstances surrounding my rescue.

That October afternoon on Burn Ward 13B, I had just finished eating lunch and was pondering my only options, watching another "soap" or taking a nap. Glancing up from my bed, I noticed a corpsmen on his way off the ward. My bed was the last one on the right. Taking a slight detour, he approached me and asked, "Hi, Captain Burk, how ya, doing?"

"Who the hell are you?"

"I'm Specialist Beaver, and it's good to see you doing so well now."

This was my first cogent conversation with Specialist 6th-Class Beaver. He was the Army corpsmen who had been on board the C-141 Starlifter which transported me from Hamilton Air Force Base to San Antonio, Texas.

During the next thirty minutes, our conversation detailed the events surrounding the flight from Travis Air Force Base to Hamilton Air Force Base on that hazy Monday morning, May 4, 1970. Specialist Beaver was the person who accepted the call from the hospital official at Hamilton. The caller explained their attempts to secure a plane to fly me to the burn unit.

"Okay," he told them, "I'll ask the crew to top off the tanks and we'll be over within thirty minutes and pick him up."

The Air Force C-141 Starlifter is aptly named. Its missions of mercy were conducted by "stars" who "lifted" GI's from danger to take them to a nearby hospital.

During my visits with Specialist Beaver, Dr. Inge, my wife and the others involved in the accident investigation, the realization of my good fortune slowly became apparent to me. After hearing how the C-141 Starlifter just "happened" to be on the ground at Travis Air Force Base, I was struck with the series of unlikely events that resulted in my life being spared.

The more I thought about it, the more it was apparent to me that a series of miraculous events had taken place: John Davieau's "accidental" discovery of me on fire in a field and extinguishing the fire on my body, the securing of the C-141 Starlifter at Travis Air Force Base, California, on a re-fueling stop and Dr. Inge being next in line to accept a new patient. All of these events reinforce my belief there were strong, unseen forces which intervened on my behalf.

I felt as if Dr. Inge being assigned as my primary care physician was not a coincidence. Dr. Inge made a commitment to me and my family. He is a wonderful doctor and a genuine caring human being; his extraordinary caring made a critical difference to me and my family throughout my stay in the hospital.

I felt as if I was reassembling a large puzzle—and a key piece would only be understood by finding the Mangel's Ranch and John Davieau.

My first meeting with John and Pearl Davieau and their daughter Laurie occurred in June, 1974.

In 1974, I was working as a civilian employee for the Air Force at Richards-Gebaur AFB, Missouri. During this time the United Stated began ceding the civilian and military control of the Ryukyu Islands, of which Okinawa was a part, to Japan. My position as an air traffic control specialist required that I travel frequently to inspect selected military air traffic control installations and assist with the development and implementation of new radar equipment.

I was scheduled for a trip to Okinawa, Japan, to help ensure the efficient and effective transfer of operational control of the Okinawa Radar Approach Control Facility (RAPCON) to the nation of Japan. I rearranged my travel schedule to Okinawa so I could spend a weekend in the Napa, California, area attempting to find the Davieaus and the Mangel's Ranch. Prior to leaving, I contacted Ray Neilsen, a former civilian employee at Hamilton AFB, California, and explained the purpose of my trip—to find the Davieaus.

During our brief phone call, I asked Ray if he would meet me at San Francisco International Airport. Ray agreed and said he was eager to see me again.

On the day of my arrival in San Francisco, Ray met me at the airport and we immediately drove to his home in Sonoma, California. Enroute to his home, Ray had a lot of questions about my health, the crash and how I was feeling. I was eager to share with him many of the details about the crash, my family, and my job at Richards-Gebaur. He was gracious and gratified that I was willing to share so much of this personal detail with him. Seeing Ray also gave me the chance to thank him for his cards and prayers.

At his home that evening, I told Ray how important it was to me to find John Davieau so I could thank him for saving my life, but I didn't know the location of the Mangel's Ranch and only had one picture of Mr. Davieau. That picture, which I still have today, shows John wearing his straw cowboy hat, denim jacket and glasses.

Ray indicated that he thought he knew the ranch's location and that we could get started early the next morning after a good night's sleep.

The next morning broke sunny and clear. Ray and I ate breakfast, jumped into his car and started driving towards Napa, California. My excitement was slowly building in anticipation of finally meeting the man who had found me and saved my life.

Our first few hours proved fruitless. At every stop, the people we asked had either never heard of the Mangel's Ranch or didn't know the location. I was getting a bit discouraged but was determined that, even if it took all that day or the next, I would find John Davieau.

Early that afternoon, tired and discouraged, we decided to eat lunch and stopped at a small Mom and Pop café on the outskirts of Napa. During lunch, Ray continued to quiz me about the crash, how I was discovered and the cause of the crash. We also had time to talk about our mutual acquaintances from Hamilton and their families.

After we finished our meal, we sat at the counter discussing our planned route. When I mentioned the Mangel's Ranch, our waitress walked over to us.

"Did I hear you say that you are looking for the Mangel's Ranch?" she asked.

"Yes Ma'am," I replied. "Do you know where it's located?"

"Yes I do," she said and then provided us detailed instructions on how to get to the ranch.

Pumped and excited, we paid our bill, thanked the waitress for her help, got back into Ray's car and, following the woman's instructions, started our drive to find the ranch.

We headed east towards the center of Napa, drove around the circle in downtown and headed south on a two-lane blacktop road. Driving south out of Napa, the surrounding countryside looked familiar to me.

Then it hit me like a flash! This was the same road I had driven several times while stationed at Hamilton enroute to the wine country in the Napa Valley. It all started rushing back to me.

"This is just too bizarre," I said to Ray. "I've been up this road a number of times."

Ray's silence was, I think, a testimony to the strange issues surrounding the accident and my rescue.

As we continued down the road, our conversation centered on the weather, our families and my good fortune, all the while continuing to search for any signs or indications of the Mangel's Ranch.

As we entered a large section of tall eucalyptus trees bordering both sides of the road, the feeling of *deja vue* overwhelmed me. Just then, glancing to my right, I noticed a large sign a few yards off the road in a nearby field.

"Stop, Ray!" I yelled. The car's brakes and tires squealed on the road surface.

"What's wrong?" he asked

"I think we just found the ranch," I said. "Back up so I can take a closer look at the sign that's just inside this fence line."

Ray put the car in reverse and we backed up slowly until the sign was again visible from the road.

"Welcome to the Mangel's Ranch, John and Pearl Davieau—Managers," the sign read.

Without hesitating, Ray changed gears and we drove slowly through the open gate and down a grass driveway towards the farmhouse.

As Ray drove the car slowly into the large yard over tire furrows impressed in the soil, I was overcome with emotion. Feeling an equal mixture of joy and anxiety, I knew I was about to cry.

My heart was pulsating in my chest, my face became flushed with excitement, and I couldn't swallow. I felt like a hand was around my throat, restricting the airflow into my lungs.

Inside the car, all was quiet except for the sound of tires slowly rolling over small rocks, soft dirt and an occasional tree branch.

We rode on the path until we were about thirty yards from the ranchhouse. Ray stopped the car and turned off the ignition. At that moment, we both saw a young girl run down from the berm above and behind the house, open the screen door and disappear inside.

"I'll wait for you here," Ray said.

I opened the passenger's side door and started to get out. I climbed slowly out of the car and started walking towards the house, thinking that someone must have heard us approach or seen me exit the car. Today, some twenty-four years after that first meeting, I can still recall the sound the screen door made as it closed.

As I approached the house, my throat became tighter, I was sweating, and my heart felt as if it were about to jump out of my chest. I was experiencing happiness and was also on the verge of tears, nervous that I was about to meet the man who had saved my life.

I walked to within a few feet of the screen door, thinking that someone, perhaps the young girl we saw a few minutes earlier, would appear at the door and greet me. No one appeared at the screen door, so I decided to walk up the sloping hill behind the house where I could see someone working on a truck. I walked slowly up the hill and stopped approximately fifteen yards away from the man who was working on the engine of his pick-up truck. It was a bright, sunny afternoon, one that required a person to wear sunglasses. The bright California sun was behind me and starting to set in the west.

"Mr. Davieau?" I asked, clearing my throat.

The man working on his truck raised up, placed his wire framed glasses on his face, grabbed a red rag wiped his hands.

"Yes," he said, squinting into the bright afternoon sun.

"I'm John Davieau. Can I help you?"

"Mr. Davieau, do you know who I am?" I asked, my emotions starting to boil over.

He paused as if he wanted to believe it was me but didn't want to ask for fear his hopes would be dashed.

"Mr. Davieau," I continued, "the last time you saw me I was on fire."

He paused for a brief second, then raced over to me, grabbed hold of me in a bear hug and started to cry.

"The last time I saw you, you were on fire," he sobbed. "I thought I'd never see you alive."

We both stood there for several minutes hugging and crying.

"Pearl, Pearl, Pearl, come quick! It's Captain Burk! It's Captain Burk!" he yelled down to the farmhouse.

Out of the corner of my right eye, I saw two women emerge from the farmhouse, take a wide, arcing turn to their left and, as fast as they could, run up the hill. They also grabbed me in a warm embrace.

All four of us stood on the crest of the small hill, in a tight embrace, jumping up and down, laughing, crying and collectively enjoying our good fortune.

"You're alive! You're alive!" Mrs. Davieau sobbed.

The feeling inside me was indescribable; my body felt like the sun—warm and radiant all over.

After embracing for several minutes, we regained our composure and walked back down the hill to the farmhouse and continued our visit. As we entered the farmhouse, I excused myself and walked over to Ray's car.

"Ray, I'm going to stay here for a few days," I said.

"I'll call you on Saturday. We can discuss when you should pick me up then. Is that okay with you?"

"Hey, George," Ray replied, through tears of his own, "I'm really glad you finally got to meet the Davieaus. I'll wait for your call on Saturday. Have a great time."

Ray drove away and I entered the ranchhouse and plopped down in a chair, teary-eyed, exhausted and totally elated. We spent the next several minutes visiting, then "Mom" Davieau showed me the spare bedroom and where to shower. After I showered, I walked back into the kitchen and noted that something delicious-smelling was cooking in a pot on the stove.

"What's that you're cooking, Mrs. Davieau?" I asked.

"Venison stew," she replied. "It's for dinner."

"Smells good," I said, "and I'm hungry!"

"Would you like something to drink?" Mr. Davieau asked.

"Yes," I replied. "What do you have?"

"Ice water, iced tea, and I have some Jack Daniels I've been saving for a special occasion," he replied. "And this," he continued, "is about as good a special occasion as I can think of."

George Burk with Pearl and John Davieu

We all gathered around the kitchen table, ate dinner, and Mr. Davieau and I drank some Jack Daniels. I spent the remainder of the day and evening getting to know the Davieau family.

The next morning, I woke up with a headache and my mouth felt like the entire Russian Army had marched through it barefoot. Yuk!

After I read the sports section of the paper, I showered, shaved, and walked back into the kitchen. Mr. and Mrs. Davieau and Laurie were up and starting their daily chores. Later that morning, we returned to the site of the crash—closure, I think the experts call it. The drive over rough, rock-strewn pasture land in his 4-wheel-drive truck took an hour even on this clear, sunny day.

John Davieu and George Burk

When we arrived, I spent an hour walking around the site, remembering the crash and the surroundings. I asked Mr. Davieau questions about exactly where it was he found me, what he remembered, and how he felt.

When we were ready to leave, I said a prayer aloud to my friends.

"I love you guys!" I yelled.

As we prepared to leave, I noticed a small vase of flowers off to our right about thirty yards away, lying at the base of one of the eucalyptus trees.

"Whose flowers?" I asked.

"One of the wives has brought them up here the past few years," he said.

"Do you know who it was?" I asked.

"No, I don't," he replied, "but I think she was Japanese; she hardly spoke any English."

"Hmm," I said. "Bet that was Fred Adam's wife. She was Japanese, and I know she spoke very little English."

"Well," he said, "every May 4th since the crash, she has come to the house and asked permission to place flowers at the spot where the plane crashed."

According to the Davieaus, this ceremony continued for several more years. Then one day they realized the Japanese lady hadn't returned. As far as I know, Mrs. Adams returned to her family in Japan in the mid-1970's.

The two days I spent visiting the Davieaus were an enjoyable and rewarding time for me. We talked and talked, ate pizza—no more Jack Daniels—and I even met one of the volunteer firefighters, one of first rescuers on the scene.

On Saturday afternoon, the Davieaus drove me to the Gulf Station in Napa, where the volunteer firefighter was employed. I can't recall his name but it too was an emotional reunion.

Another firefighter who responded to the crash, and with whom I correspond every Christmas, is Richard St. Laurent. His friends call him "The Saint."

Mr. St. Laurent is seventy-four years young now, still works full-time, and he and his lovely red-headed wife reside in Sonoma, California. Two more "heroes" who made a difference in my life.

The visit with the Davieaus helped me close a few psychological wounds and erase the lingering doubt I had about whether a person really did find me. The visit also helped me climb another plateau on my road to recovery and to move on with my life.

The Davieaus are now retired and live in Sudan, Texas. Dr. Inge is still practicing medicine in Dover, Delaware. Every Christmas since 1971, I have arranged to have a package of baklava sent to them.

The baklava is but a small token of my appreciation, esteem, respect and love for the people most responsible for saving my life.

The Davieaus and I visit on the phone quite often. Mrs. Davieau attended a conference where I was the keynote speaker in Lubbock, Texas, in January, 1997, and I have seen them, their daughters, Patti, Shelly, and Laurie, several times since our first meeting in 1974.

Over the years since the crash, Mr. Davieau has often said to me, "Captain, I know God sent me to find you." You know what else? I believe him!

Dr. Inge always acknowledges his receipt of my Christmas gift with a letter. In his letters, he often says that it seems hard to believe it has been so many years since the accident, and he is glad to know I continue to do so well.

In his letter of December 21, 1994, he said, "I think most kindly of you and have frequently recalled the story you related to me about not going across the bridge with your colonel and therefore feeling that your life was saved by staying on the other side of the bridge."

Twenty-four years from the date of the accident and he still remembers my story!

Chapter Ten: Starlifter C-141

"There are no accidents. Everything that happens has a purpose."   James Redfield

The events leading to my arrival at the burn unit in San Antonio unfolded over time as a tale of remarkable timing, good luck and unbelievable coincidence.

Our country's military involvement in Southeast Asia had resulted in unique types of injuries not seen during previous military conflicts. Many of the GI's who were burned in the jungles of Southeast Asia suffered severe phosphorous burns to all parts of the body. The nature and extent of the injuries, combined with improved medical care and the means to transport injured GI's to the rear areas, created more and more survivors requiring specialized care. The hospitals in Vietnam and the hospital ships moored nearby offshore lacked both the staff and capacity to handle the number of injuries, and the injuries were still increasing. The need to transport the injured to state-side hospitals was paramount.

The decision was made at the Department of the Army, Washington, DC, to schedule regular flights from the Far East to hospitals in the states. Starting in 1965, an Army Burn Team would fly on a commercial aircraft from San Antonio, Texas, to Tachikawa Air Force Base, Japan, via Seattle, Washington. After arriving in Japan, the Burn Team would meet and board an Air Force C-141 Starlifter, for the flight to San Antonio. The standard flight plan was to depart Japan on a Monday morning, cross the international date line, and land at Travis Air Force Base the same day at approximately nine o'clock in the morning. The plane and crew landed at Travis Air Force Base to take on additional fuel and provide a brief rest for the crew.

From 1965 until early 1975, this trip was made twice a month on alternate Mondays. The C-141 Starlifter landed at Travis Air Force the morning of May, 4th, 1970—the day of my crash.

After the crash and my rescue, the hospital staff at Hamilton Air Force base attempted to locate an airplane to fly me to San Antonio and the burn unit. Calls were made to locations throughout the western part of the United States but to no avail. Aircraft that were available were either too far away to help or not the type of aircraft needed. The last call made by a member of the Hamilton Air Force Base hospital staff was to Base Operations at Travis Air Force Base.

The dispatcher at Base Operations accepted the call, was advised of the crash and told that the sole survivor needed transportation to San Antonio. The dispatcher, when asked if another plane was available at Travis, replied, "Stand-by one," and contacted a member of the burn team onboard the plane. A few seconds later, Specialist Beaver rushed into Base Operations and was handed the phone.

The hospital representative told Specialist Beaver the nature and extent of my burns and internal injuries and requested the aircraft be diverted to Hamilton. Specialist Beaver hung up the phone, raced across the tarmac to the airplane and advised the aircraft commander and the medical staff they had another stop. He told the medical staff on board about the nature and extent of my injuries and made ready for their departure from Travis AFB.

Refueling the C-141 was completed quickly, and the plane departed to Hamilton, arriving approximately thirty minutes later. Approximately four hours after I was placed on board the plane at Hamilton, we arrived in San Antonio.

The marvel in this story is that had the C-141 aircraft been a few minutes earlier arriving at Travis Air Force base, its departure would have been earlier, making my transport to San Antonio impossible to complete.

The C-141 arrived at Travis shortly after the crash occurred. If the call had not been made to Travis, my life would not have been spared. If the C-141 had arrived at Travis on any other day but a Monday, I would not be here.

I have come to believe more strongly that this whole series of events, including the plane refueling at Travis Air Force base that Monday morning must be more than coincidence. All of this leaves me with a sense that there is some hidden meaning to my life, some important reason that I am still alive.

Chapter Eleven: ICU

"We are not our tapes."   **Ken Keyes**

My three-month stay in the ICU was long and torturous. Numerous internal and external blood and skin infections and other complications, any one of which could have been fatal by itself, were expected to terminate my life. I had thirty major surgeries, six minor operations, seventy-six pints of blood, seven units of plasma, and six units of platelets. My initial physical therapy required me to relearn things I had previously accepted as routine. Simple acts like standing, walking, eating, going to the bathroom, and the physical and mental acts of transitioning from a left-handed to right-handed person were my immediate challenges.

Finally, in late August 1970, Dr. Inge had me moved from the ICU to the main ward, Ward 14A. I spent the next four weeks in a drug-induced stupor. All the events and people that surrounded me are a blur. Specific events which happened during that time don't seem real. It's like a continuation of my dream or nightmare. One of the few things I recall is hollering at one of the guys lying across from my rotating bed.

Our electric rotating beds obstructed our view of each other but that was only a minor irritant. We didn't let it deter us from lobbing obscenities across the aisles at each other and the nurses. It was our way of trying to ease the pain, discomfort and fear.

I'd also try to identify the various sounds from outside the hospital - sounds I knew as familiar before my injuries. Somehow it was impossible now to connect them with anything familiar.

"Is that a lawn mower outside?" I'd ask a corpsmen.

"Yes," he'd reply.

Then my mind would try to recall the smell of freshly cut grass.

"Is it raining outside?" I'd ask.

"Yes," would be the reply.

Trying unsuccessfully to remember the smell of the air after a rain caused me to be more frustrated and anxious. I was furious at myself for not being able to recall these simple sounds and smells.

My attempts to recall other experiences, like the sound of pigeons cooing, the smell of fresh flowers, birds singing and snow crunching under my feet, were fruitless. All the sights and sounds taken for granted the first twenty-nine years of my life were unrecognizable. Just when I needed them.

In late September 1970, Dr. Inge transferred me a second time. This time it was downstairs to Ward 13B, or "The Hilton," as we called it.

Patients were moved to the ward to await further surgeries as their physical condition improved and their physical survival was relatively assured. Ward 13B was to be my home for the next fourteen months.

Part of my physical rehabilitation required me to stand next to my bed for a few minutes several times a day. Standing was extremely difficult and painful. My legs felt as if they were on fire; they burned and itched simultaneously. The burns and skin grafts on my legs required me to wear support stockings from my ankles to my groin. The stockings kept the skin grafts in place and provided support for my legs. Even while wearing the support hose (I called them my menopause hose), my legs felt like they would explode.

The thin skin and grafts created an intense itching and burning sensation, and bending my right arm was impossible. My right arm was restricted by calcium deposits that had developed in the elbow joint while I was lying motionless on my right side for three weeks in the ICU. I had to stay still so that the grafting on my lower back could heal. My lack of mobility and my diet, rich in vitamins and minerals, froze my arm at the elbow joint.

The deposits were surgically removed in November, 1970. After the surgery, my right arm was encased in a dynamic splint for two months. The splint forced my arm to bend at the elbow and prevented the calcium deposits from returning. This was painful and distracting, but it seems now a small price to pay for more freedom.

My first meal on the ward after the surgery was Thanksgiving dinner. I ate turkey, stuffing and all the trimmings. Having the mobility in my elbow to feed myself made the food taste even better.

The majority of the patients on the ward were GI's burned in Vietnam and neighboring countries in Southeast Asia. Many suffered phosphorous burns which are particularly painful and often leave more scarring than a more typical burn. Several of my friends had their arms, legs, or both amputated.

Of all the guys on the ward during this time, several stand out in my mind. One was Bob Hameras. Bob was a Captain in the US Army. He was burned when President Nixon approved the movement of troops into Laos and Cambodia in the fall of 1970. Bob was burned while on a patrol with his squad when they were ambushed by North Vietnamese regulars. As a result of the ensuing fire fight, he sustained second- and third-degree phosphorous burns on his legs, hands and back.

When I was feeling strong enough or was bored with too much television or sleeping, I'd visit Bob and try to cheer him up. During my first visit, Bob was startled when he opened his eyes and saw me standing at his bedside.

"Good morning, how ya doing," I asked. "Do you want some orange juice?"

"Uh!" he grunted, meaning "yes."

"Do you want some cereal?" I asked again,

"Uh," he grunted again.

After a few more questions and a corresponding number of grunts, I told Bob, "Listen up buddy. You can shove your attitude right up your a__! If you want to lay there and die, go ahead. Waste someone else's time."

Then I shuffled back to my bed, climbed in, pulled the sheet over me and went back to sleep.

Bob Hameras spent all of his time in bed. The only time he would move was when the corpsmen would physically lift him out of bed to change his bed linens. We all knew Bob's emotional state at that time because his depression, anger and fear were emotions all of us experienced. Because Bob didn't make any effort to help with his own care, the corpsmen making his bed had to lift him off his bed and place him on a portable cart or gurney.

After making his bed and replacing the soiled sheets and pillow cases, the corpsmen lifted Bob off the cart and returned him to bed. This exercise, repeated day after day, was obviously tiring and frustrating for the corpsmen. Watching this process repeated for over a month enhanced my respect for them and their commitment to us.

But their growing frustration and anger towards Bob's attitude was apparent and understandable. They were angry at a man who was giving up and dying a little bit more each day.

The assistance Bob needed resided within himself. Until and unless he made the choice to live and work through the physical and emotional pain and doubt he was facing, his demise was almost certain.

It isn't a pretty sight, watching someone give up and die a little bit each day. Yet there was nothing anyone could do for him. Bob had to find his own "why" to live, then he could endure almost any "how."

Dying is easy, sometimes it's the living which is difficult. Many people complain that they don't have enough time to do what they want to do. Yet, to someone who is in physical pain or overwhelming emotional anguish, time—and life—can be a burden.

Bob didn't have many visitors, and that was the primary reason he was quitting on himself. One constant for most of us on the ward was that we all knew the importance of family and friends. People who love you stand with you and encourage you, especially when encouragement is needed the most.

Except for an occasional grunt, Bob seldom talked to any of us. When someone stopped at his bed to say hello, his standard reply was his deep, garbled "uh."

Our joint attempts to yell and cheer him up were fruitless. If Bob was going to live and find purpose in his life, he would have to find it for himself.

Finally, we simply ignored him because of our unwritten code.

There was an unwritten code of conduct among all the guys on the ward. No matter how down a person was or how much pain they experienced, a patient couldn't fool anyone else because there was always someone enduring more pain.

The "poor me" syndrome was not tolerated, but we supported each other through various emotional and physical crises and post-operational blues.

Soliciting sympathy or pity from family, friends, nurses or even the doctors often was successful but didn't work with the other burn survivors. Family and friends, not having a right to do otherwise, often let patients get away with self-pity.

Bob's situation was an example of how a negative attitude could directly lead to a person's slow physical and emotional deterioration. Bob remained on his back for so long that an ulcer developed on his lower back, just above his tailbone.

A week after my first visit with Bob, and after visits by several other patients, our struggles to get him up and moving appeared to pay dividends. One morning, Bob started moving his arms and legs. His pain and discomfort were apparent in his screams. We continued to encourage him, telling him he'd feel better tomorrow than today and to keep working.

Several days later, we were surprised to see Bob try to sit up in bed and feed himself. When six of us in nearby beds saw this, we started hooting and hollering at him. Several of the nurses, hearing the commotion, thought something bad had occurred.

"What's wrong, what's wrong?" several of the nurses asked as they raced into the ward.

"Awe nothing," was the reply. "Old Bob is finally getting his lazy rear-end out of bed and getting with the program."

A few days later, the change in Bob's attitude was even more apparent. At last, it appeared that he wanted to recover and get out of the hospital.

One week later, with assistance from two corpsmen, Bob struggled to get out of bed for the first time in months and stood next to his bed. Several days later, he attended his first physical therapy session. This was a major milestone in his recovery because the physical therapists were located off the ward.

Walking to his therapy with assistance from our corpsmen was no easy task, and it took a lot of courage and mental strength for Bob to work through the physical pain.

Bob was a living image of a skinny, white scarecrow. He was like a human skeleton with patches of red and white skin draped over the bones. Wearing black low-cut brogan boots lined with lamb's wool and supported by parallel bars, he was literally learning how to walk again. A nurse standing nearby yelled encouragement to him.

Approximately seven months later, Bob was released from the hospital and received a medical retirement from the Army. He returned to his home near Los Angeles, California, to complete his recovery. I've had no further contact with him and hope he continues to enjoy a healthy, happy and productive life.

Another person whose situation didn't turn out as well was an Army Captain who occupied the electric bed to my right on Ward 14A. We didn't have the time, energy or mental capacity to know one another's names. All of us were heavily sedated with morphine and hiding away in the far reaches of our minds where pain, discomfort and other realities were distant.

Information told to us seconds earlier drifted rapidly from reach, and it was impossible to recall names, addresses, and other facts that should have been immediately accessible. This lack of ability to grasp information exacerbated our emotional and physical distress.

The time of day, day of the week, children's names—simple everyday details of life that normal people could remember—were impossible for us to recite.

One day, while still in the ever-present rotating electric hospital bed, I opened my eyes from one of my drug-induced stupors and noticed an unfamiliar odor, distinctly different from the now-familiar smell of burned and destroyed flesh covered in white gauze and sulfamylon cream. Trying to determine the source of the smell was difficult. My first thought was that it must be me who smelled so bad, so I just dismissed it as my body odor. I had better things to think about, like trying to make the pain disappear.

Well, the smell didn't go away and, in fact, increased in its intensity. A few hours—or was it minutes?—later, standing near my bed, I overheard a team of doctors talking about the guy lying in the electric bed immediately to my right. They were talking about amputating part of one arm because of gangrene. After hearing that, the strange smell made sense to me.

The patient in that bed was an Army Captain, burned in a plane crash in "Nam". He appeared to have family visit him daily. In fact, every time I opened my eyes, and looked down at the foot of my bed, I saw three, four, even five people standing or seated at the foot of his bed. It wasn't their appearance which made me angry, but it was what they were doing, or rather what they were not doing.

I couldn't hear what they were saying, but whatever it was it must have had a dire affect on their son and brother.

Between sobs and wails of grief, I heard voices bemoan the fact that he was burned and injured.

Over the next few days—or was it hours?—several of us started hollering at the people to "shut the hell up" and imploring the nurses and corpsmen to get them out of there.

"I don't need to hear this shit," I kept telling myself and the nurses.

Then, just as quickly as the visits began, the ward was once again quiet except for the heavy breathing, gagging, screams and moaning of the patients. That noise was accepted and understood. The unusual interruptions to our normal routines had gone away.

Several weeks later, Dr. Inge transferred me downstairs to the "Hilton," Ward 13B. My bed was the first bed on the left in the ward.

One afternoon, after lunch was served and I was contemplating taking a nap, the sound and vibration of a bed rolling quickly down the marble floor distracted me. The sound grew louder and louder.

Suddenly, off to my right, I saw a bed flash by me being pushed down the aisle to the rear of the ward to the Renal Lab. A corpsman was pushing the bed; riding on the head board, with her feet between the metal head board and her hands around the face of the patient was Captain Myra Peche.

Myra was one of my ICU nurses.

As the bed moved quickly past my line of sight, I noticed that she was squeezing a black bulb attached to the patient's throat. Small patches of blood were splattered on the sheet and on Myra's white plastic gloves. The black bulb she was squeezing forced air into the patient's lungs and helped him breathe.

"I've seen that damn thing before," I thought.

"In the tank when Dr. Inge was cutting away my skin. Myra was the one holding the bulb then too."

"That looks like the Army Captain who was in the bed next to me upstairs," I thought.

I quickly dismissed the incident as my imagination and went to sleep.

Sleeping remained a challenge as I could only lie on my back. At this point, I had lost over a hundred pounds and only weighed 125 pounds. I couldn't get comfortable turned on either side as there was no muscle to pad the bones, and my shoulders were still too weak to accept any weight.

I managed to doze off and imagined myself standing, walking, eating, going to the bathroom myself and walking out of the hospital. Dreams were always part of my psyche. I was "visualizing" or mind-mapping as a way to help my mind heal my body and was still able to build my "pup tents" against the cruel incursion of reality.

Later that afternoon, as I lay in bed watching a game show on TV, I noticed Myra Peche walking down the aisle to leave the ward. She looked exhausted, like someone had pulled her through a keyhole. Her stride was slow, her shoulders slouched, and the white surgical mask hung from around her neck in front of her throat.

I noticed her glancing at me, probably checking to see if I was awake.

"Hey Myra," I said. "I figured that was you I saw earlier on that bed."

"Yeah, that was me," she said, her voice cracking with emotion and frustration. "How are you doing?" she asked, approaching my bed

"Fine," I replied. "Was that the Army Captain who was next to me upstairs that you took to the back of the ward?"

"Yeah, it was him," she responded. "We took him back to the Renal Lab. All his systems were shutting down."

"Well, how is he doing?" I asked.

Myra paused, as if trying to capture the right words.

"Well, he just died," she released, her voice reflecting a great deal of emotion and frustration.

"No!" she said, pausing to catch herself. "He didn't die, he quit."

Instinctively, we both knew what she meant. No further explanation was necessary.

Myra, along with Sheri McGhee, was part of the team of nurses who pleaded, cajoled, screamed, endured my complaining, and did whatever else they could to keep me alive during my eighty-nine day stay in the ICU.

"I'm exhausted," she said. "I'm going home," and leaned over my bed and kissed me on the cheek.

"Thanks again, Myra," I said. "Say hello to Sheri for me. I love you guys."

"He quit, gave up," I thought. "Hell, I know why. His family gave him nothing to fight for. All that crying and wailing at his bed just enabled him to leave. I know what he was probably thinking in his mind," I thought. "He reached up with his index finger, grabbed the window shade and pulled the shade down."

I imagined his last subconscious thoughts as something like, "Hey, I don't need this crap, I'm outta here."

To this day, I am convinced that the ultimate cause of his death wasn't the obvious destruction of his body by burns and related diseases. It was the breakdown of his will to live and his failure to see a reason "why". He just gave up because he was disappointed by his family's negative reaction to him and his injuries. They were unwilling to support him in finding a "why" to live, and he chose not to find the "how" in his life.

If he had been unable or unwilling to fight for his life and not give up, his family had an opportunity and an obligation to help him find a "why" for his life so he could bear the terrible "how" of his existence as a burn victim.

That purpose could help him make the transformation from victim to a survivor.

The journey from victim to survivor begins with self-analysis, forgiveness, and the realization and understanding of the "why" in our lives. We need to learn to listen to God and discover our purpose: a goal to achieve, a birthday to celebrate, a child and family to see, a meal to eat, a hug from a parent and spouse, a book to write. When a person does not see any more sense in his life, no aim, no mission or purpose, and therefore no point in carrying on, he soon is lost!

We are being questioned and challenged by life every hour of every day. A big part of that challenge is accepting responsibility for our actions, being accountable and conducting ourselves in a way which brings respect and admiration to us and our families.

In addition to the Army Captain, I know two men who shared time and space with me on the ward who committed suicide. Both suicides occurred several years after their release from the hospital and further illustrates their unwillingness to accept the uniqueness of their suffering.

All of us have crosses to bear. How we carry that cross is a true measure of who we are as people. Many of us realize that perhaps it is our destiny to suffer. It is our task. Our suffering is unique in the world and no one can relieve us of that burden. Our challenges lie in the manner in which we bear that cross; only with God's guidance are we able to achieve our purpose.

Many of us cried lots of tears about this strange set of circumstances in which we found ourselves. However, we were not ashamed of crying, as our tears and the tears of our families bore witness to the greatest courage of all, the courage to suffer.

Chapter Twelve: The Porch

"I'm not okay; you're not okay; and that's okay."
                              Virginia Satir

On a clear, sunny day in March, 1971, while I was in a half-asleep state, Dr. Tom Newsome, my backup physician, stopped at my bed to visit. After exchanging the usual greetings, he inquired about my overall health, asked if I liked the accommodations, and then told me the purpose of his visit.

Dr. Newsome said a new patient had been brought down to 13B from 14A the night before and was in a floating bed in the room in the front part of the ward across from the nurses' station. He explained that the patient, an Army Captain and helicopter pilot, was shot down in Vietnam and received third degree burns to his face and right arm. Dr. Newsome asked if I would take a few minutes and visit him.

"Why me, Doc?" I asked.

"Why not you?" he said. "You have overcome so much and have such a positive attitude. Perhaps you can boost his spirits. You both have something in common. You're officers and plane crash survivors."

"Well, Doc," I replied with some doubt in my mind, " I'll think about it."

Our visit over, Dr. Newsome said goodbye and hurriedly returned to complete his morning rounds.

"That's the last thing I want to do," I thought. "I've got better things to do with my time."

The surgery on my left stub and the grafting required made me a bit edgy. My patience was a bit thin. I was tired and needed to recuperate from the recent surgery. I was determined to get some sleep, so I climbed back into bed under the bird cage and closed my eyes.

Several hours later, while under the bird cage, my conscience started getting the best of me. The bird cage, a series of horizontal and vertical metal strips shaped to fit over a patient's body, is placed over the patient while he is lying in bed, and a sheet is draped over the cage. This keeps the sheets from rubbing against the newly grafted skin and donor sites so they can heal, and at the same time the patient can stay warm.

My inner voice kept telling me to stop being so damned selfish, get my rear-end out of bed and go visit this "new guy."

"Watching another game show or soap opera is boring," I thought. "Why not visit this guy. Hey, if others had the same attitude about me, I might not be alive."

I lay in bed for another few minutes struggling with my conscience. "Oh, what the hell," I thought, and turned to my right, pushed the nurses' call button and waited for a nurse to help me out of bed.

A few minutes later, "Granny", one of our civilian nurses, walked to my bed and removed the sheets from the cage.

"Yes, Captain?" she asked. "What do you need?"

"I'm going to visit the new guy Dr. Newsome told me about this morning," I replied. "I need your help getting out of bed."

"Okay," she said, "let's get you out of here and on your way."

Granny helped me out of bed, placed my feet in my blue cotton slippers and pulled my pajama bottoms up to the donor site on my lower left abdomen. After Granny tied my pajama bottoms, I held my left stub above my head to reduce the pain and started walking to where the new patient was located.

As I entered the small room across from the nurses' station, I noticed that all the beds, except one, were empty. The low light level created an eerie feeling in the room and the stillness was interrupted only by the bubbling and gurgling sound from a silicone bed to my right and just inside the doorway.

The staff placed the bed so it couldn't easily be seen from the hallway. As I approached the bed, an uneasy, sinking feeling hit me in the stomach. I glanced cautiously at one end of the silicone bed, apprehensive at what I was probably going to see. The part of the body I saw first was a head, or what my mind told me was a head. The only smell in the room was the ever-present aroma of burned flesh and sulfamylon cream. My instinct told me to get the hell outta there!

Glancing down at him, I wished I had listened to my instincts. What I saw in the bed was a man without a face. My eyes must have been playing tricks on me because they didn't believe what my mind was seeing. There he was, Captain John Smith (a pseudonym), US Army, shot down in Vietnam. He had no face. Where there was supposed to be a nose, all that remained were two small holes between his eyes. One ear was gone and one-half of the other ear was missing and his mouth was wide open.

"Wait a minute," I thought. "Damn, his mouth isn't open. He has no mouth!"

John's mouth and surrounding facial tissue were so badly burned that most of his jaw was gone.

"Well, that's enough of this crap," I thought. "I don't need this s_ _ _! No way in hell I'm going to sit and look at him." I turned around and started to return to the safety of my bed.

As I shuffled out of that room, my conscious and sub-conscious mind continued to try and grasp what my eyes had seen.

"Man, oh man!" I thought, "How can the nurses and corpsmen look at him? The guy's a real mess."

"Is anyone there?" a barely audible voice gurgled.

"What are you gonna do now, you jerk?" I thought.

One thing I knew for certain: my desire to leave that room far surpassed any desire to stay and visit with him.

"I don't need this," I thought again and returned to my bed on the main ward.

I climbed into bed, asked a corpsmen to rearrange my bird cage and cover it with a sheet to help keep me warm. Thinking about the severity of John's injuries was the last on my things-to-do list.

"Hmm," I thought, "wonder what's on television?"

Although my body surface suffered more extensive burns than John's, my face was not as severely burned as his face. In fact, there was little comparison. Drifting off to sleep, my thoughts once again shifted to my family, leaving the hospital, and creating more pup tents. Sleep was once again a welcome friend. Was my conscience bothering me? Probably.

Several hours later, I heard a soft whimpering from a nearby bed. I opened my eyes and discovered one of the younger patients was crying. His cries rapidly became loud wails and sobbing.

"Hey dude," I said. "What's wrong?"

"My wife hasn't been here for a week," he said. "She went back home."

Then, at the top of his lungs, he screamed that he just wanted to die, that no one cared about him now that he was different.

One of the nurses heard his screams, entered the room, walked to his bed and began talking to him in quiet, reassuring tones. Then she gave him a sedative to help him go to sleep.

Later the same day, the nurse told me his wife had filed for divorce and wanted custody of their only child. His wife's timing could not have been more exquisite! Unfortunately, this was not an uncommon occurrence on the burn ward.

An hour or so later, as a corpsmen changed my dressings, I asked him the time and when dinner would be served. I no sooner asked him when I saw a dinner cart roll past our area headed for the rear part of the ward.

"Maybe eating will help me forget what I've seen and let me concentrate on my issues," I said.

After dinner, my thoughts drifted back to John and to my selfish and shallow feelings about visiting him. I was ambushed by my own guilt, and it hurt.

Here I was given an opportunity to try and help another guy on the ward, but I chose to let my personal feelings interfere with what I knew was the right action to take.

"Ignoring him," I rationalized, "is the easiest and most comfortable thing to do."

"Hey," I thought. "Everyone else is ignoring him, so it's okay for you too."

Then as if hit by a lightning bolt or a message from a higher source of power, I quickly finished eating, slipped on my slippers and shuffled back to visit John.

I entered the room the second time and walked directly to the side of the floating silicone bed so John could hear my voice if, in fact, he could not see me. I knew he could see only figures, not specific facial features. I stopped at the side of his bed and waited a few seconds to see if he would respond.

"Would you like some company, John?" I asked, clearing my throat.

"Yeah, that would be nice," he said in a muffled, gurgling voice.

I pulled up a padded chair and we started to talk about our injuries, our families, where he attended college, and how he was burned. Over the next few hours, the conversation shifted from our families and mutual interests to our expectations, aspirations and goals.

During that first visit, we discovered our lives had many parallels. Our fathers were railroaders and our mothers great cooks. Then our conversation shifted to the types of women we liked, sports we played, and the beer we drank.

We both agreed how great a cold bottle of beer would taste and other, more intimate, discussions about women and sex. We liked them both with equal enthusiasm.

Our visit started at seven o'clock in the evening and was interrupted only by the sound of a rolling cart loaded with sandwiches and cold drinks being shoved around the ward by a corpsmen. To our surprise, it was ten o'clock, and the nightly rounds were underway. We had lost all track of time.

Stopping by my chair, the corpsmen rattled off all the types of sandwiches and sodas he had on the cart.

"Do you want something to drink?" I asked John.

"A 7-Up," he said.

The corpsmen handed me a 7-Up, and I carefully started removing the pull tab.

"Hey, John, do you want a straw?" I asked.

John paused, then gurgled his barely audible response.

"I'm lying here like a large mouth bass and you ask me if I need a straw," he replied.

For a few seconds the room was still. The only sound was the silicone bed bubbling underneath John. Then, as if on cue, we realized what John just said and its irony. We both started chuckling, then laughing as hard as we could given our physical challenges. As we continued laughing, I lost my grip on the can of 7-UP, it fell on the marble floor and exploded into a thousand droplets of cold soda.

I saw a shadow enter the room, looked up and saw the night nurse standing in front of me with her hands on her hips and a scowl on her face.

"Are you all right?" she asked. "I thought someone fell in here."

Trying to control my laughter so the motion wouldn't irritate my left stub and fresh donor sites, I assured her everything was okay.

As we continued laughing, the nurse turned to walk away with a look that left no doubt she was telling us we were crazy. You know what? She was right. We were all a little bit crazy given our collective circumstances at the time. Our humor helped many of us through some difficult days. Assured that we were both in our right minds, the nurse walked out of the room shaking her head. I think she was chuckling to herself when she left.

After John and I stopped laughing, I rose slowly from the chair and began to leave the room and return to my bed. John tried to say something to me from a mouth that really wasn't there.

"Where are you going?" he gurgled.

"Hey," I said. "You're laughing now, buddy. You've got it made. It's all downhill from here. I'll be back tomorrow morning."

I returned the next day and over the ensuing months spent many hours with John, sharing our thoughts, aspirations and goals. To this day, even though we have limited contact, John is a true hero and a continuing source of inspiration to me.

Another patient on the ward who became a friend was Tony Borgate (a pseudonym). Tony was a 19-year-old Italian from the Bronx. After enlisting in the Army, he became a crew chief and door gunner on a UH-1, Huey helicopter. In July, 1970, Tony and his pilot were on a night mission in South Vietnam in support of US military ground forces. It was a mission that required Tony to deploy phosphorous canisters that, when ignited, can create up to one-million candle-power of light. On a particularly dangerous night mission, Tonys' helicopter, filled with phosphorous canisters, became a fiery hell when it was hit by a rocket-propelled grenade.

The RPG ignited the phosphorous canisters inside the chopper endangering Tony, his pilot and his co-pilot. Without regard to his own safety, Tony grabbed the burning canisters and began lobbing them out of the helicopter. He didn't notice that, while he was throwing the ignited phosphorous canisters out of the helicopter, the propeller wash from the helicopter blades was blowing the white hot phosphorous back on his hands, legs and face. As a result, the phosphorous burned through Tony's gloves and the front of his flight suit, severely burning his face, arms, hands and legs.

When Tony and I first met, he was blind in his left eye, had 22/100 vision in his right eye, and had sustained deep second and third degree burns on his face, arms and legs. We both occupied beds on Ward 14A for several weeks after my removal from the ICU. Several weeks after Dr.

Inge transferred me downstairs to Ward 13B, Tony followed me. He remained there for the next year until his release from the hospital and medical retirement from the Army.

Our beds on both of the wards were only a few yards apart and we spent our waking hours yelling at one another. Tony would call me a "frickin zoomie" and I'd call him a "frickin grunt." After his release from the hospital, Tony moved back to the Bronx, then to Blauvelt, New York, with his parents. They were afraid the local thugs would rob him for his Social Security and disability payments he received at their Bronx apartment.

For several years after his release from the burn unit, Tony became somewhat of a recluse. In 1981, Tony married a nurse, and they now reside in Connecticut. He is employed with the Veterans Administration and counsels other disabled veterans.

These two men are a continuing source of inspiration for me and are my heroes.

During our stay on Ward 13B, many of us discussed our burn injuries, lives and living, our dreams and our goals for after our release from the hospital. All of us agreed that the human body is an amazing machine. Under the most difficult and physiologically stressing situations, it is able to respond to many internal and external stimuli. Out of sheer necessity and will power, several of us practiced relaxation or distraction techniques to help us endure the physical and emotional challenges we faced on a minute-to-minute, hour-to-hour and day-to-day basis. Many of the older guys, in terms of age and the length of time on the ward, often shared these techniques with the new arrivals or anyone else who wanted to listen and learn.

Tony, for example, learned how to listen to footsteps approaching his bed and make a game out of identifying his mother, dad, sister, brother, doctor or nurse just from the sounds. Some of the others who had temporary or permanent hearing loss, learned to read lips. As for me, I learned a little of both and taught myself the techniques now called visualization or mind-mapping. These techniques proved an invaluable tool not only while in the hospital but after my release. Although the fog of time has eroded other incidents and discussions, I can never, nor do I want to, forget the events which pulled all of us together.

Chapter Thirteen: Stuck On My Stuff

*"If you don't do something differently, you'll end up
where you are headed."*   *Gary Koyen*

In November 1970, ten days before Thanksgiving,
calcium deposits which had formed in my elbow as a
result of excessive amounts of Vitamin D given
intravenously in the ICU, were surgically removed. These
calcium deposits caused my good arm to be frozen at the
elbow, so I was unable to feed myself.

Physical therapy started three days after the surgery
and would, it was hoped, prevent the calcium deposits
from returning. I wore a dynamic splint, except while
sleeping, showering and attending therapy. The splint
encased my entire arm from just above the wrist to just
below the shoulder, forcing my arm to bend at the elbow.
But finally, I could feed myself.

Once a day for two weeks, my arm was immersed up to
the shoulder in a small stainless steel tank filled with hot
water. The hot water allowed the elbow joint and its
surrounding tissue to warm and become relaxed. After
soaking the elbow for a few minutes in the hot water, a
corpsmen would place his hands on my right wrist and
push my hand and forearm slowly back to my right
shoulder. The pain was excruciating. Fortunately for me, I
did not feel all of the pain. Dr. Inge had prescribed a small
amount of morphine to help reduce my discomfort.

Early one afternoon, after experiencing a week of
grueling therapy, I saw Dr. Inge down the hallway at the
nurses' station and shuffled towards him.

"Hi, George," he said as I approached. "How is the
elbow therapy working out?"

"Doc, that's what I wanted to talk to you about," I replied. "The morphine or whatever you are giving me for pain for my elbow therapy just isn't cutting it. Can you increase the dosage?" I asked. "Even for me, the pain is pretty difficult to handle."

He nodded agreement, said he'd increase the dosage and assured me it would decrease my discomfort. Unknown to me, he doubled the dosage. I had absolutely no inkling what effect the increased dosage would have on me.

The next morning, I followed my usual morning routine—wake up, go to the bathroom, clean up, eat breakfast, take a nap and wait for my ten o'clock therapy session.

At nine-thirty, I pushed the nurse's call button and waited for Granny to arrive and administer the shot of morphine. A few minutes later, Granny arrived at my bed and I prepared for her to administer the shot.

"Okay, Captain, drop' em and roll," she said.

I loosened my pajama bottoms, rolled on my left side and felt the sting of the needle...and waited.

The morphine rush didn't take long. About a minute later, the extra rush of morphine pulsed through my body and enveloped me like a warm blanket. Only this time I wasn't ready for the extra kick it gave me. The sensation pulsing through my body was greater than any orgasm and lasted for a few short minutes. Then I dozed off to sleep and woke-up in the early afternoon with a terrible headache.

"My therapy session will wait until tomorrow," I thought. "I'm in no condition to walk to the elevator, never mind having 'Murph' bend my arm. What I do want is another fix."

Throughout the following day and into the night, my thoughts were focused solely on one thing—getting another shot of morphine.

"Can't that clock move faster," I thought as my agitation and nervousness increased. Time seemed to be standing still. I finally dozed off and had a restless night's sleep.

At six o'clock the next morning, I was roused from sleep by people talking in the area around my bed. I opened my eyes and saw two corpsmen shaving a patient and making him ready for surgery a few hours later.

Unable to go back to sleep, my thoughts wandered to the outside world. I looked out of the window into a gray and foggy morning (or was that my emotional state?). The decision to stay in the warmth and comfort of my bed and wait for breakfast was easy. I was just too lazy to walk to the elevator and go to the cafeteria downstairs on the main floor. Breakfast was rolled in on the food carts, and after eating a small portion of my cereal, I once again eagerly pressed the nurse's call button.

Just like the day before, the "orgasmic rush" rolled over me like a wave and drifted me away to the pain-free comfort of sleep.

The cycle of waking up and feeling physically and emotionally horrible and depressed was repeated over and over again for several weeks. My negative attitude and mental state started affecting my interaction with the other patients, my wife and the hospital staff. They had become a nuisance. I knew the morphine was controlling my life and I was hooked.

Three weeks later, while in bed one dreary Monday morning, my mind cleared of the morphine, I began to consciously think about what I was doing to myself. It was no secret. The truth about what was happening to me was becoming harder to ignore. I didn't want to know the truth; it was too painful. I could feel my self-respect and dignity being eroded away like sand on a beach. "You dumb shit," I scolded myself. "Come this far and blow it now? For what? Stop running away."

"Think about all the people who helped you get this far," I kept reminding myself. "Don't throw it all away for a few seconds of gratification."

Overcoming my dependency on morphine was a decision I had to make. I knew no one could do it for me. No more excuses, rationalizing, running away from the truth or blaming other people or the crash on my situation.

"What are you gonna do now?" I mused.

Thoughts about my future, my family and a second chance at life flashed across my mind in fast forward. The actions I had to take were as clear as a crystal ball.

The first step was admitting my dependency on morphine.

"You have a problem," I thought. "Do what needs to be done to break the cycle before it really gets the best of you."

I knew the morphine was my mask or smoke screen to help me hide from the truth about the accident, my burn injuries, and my future. Being a drug addict was not what I wanted to do with the rest of my life.

Several weeks earlier, as I read a book on stress management and overcoming fears, a quote applicable then, and even more so today, jumped off the page at me.

"Do the thing you fear the most, and the death of fear is certain."

That forced me to think about those situations which made me feel apprehensive, and it helped me to become even more determined to identify my fears, prioritize each of these fears and develop strategies to conquer them.

The second step in my strategy was to tell Dr. Inge that I didn't want any more morphine before my elbow therapy. That afternoon, during another brief visit with him, he canceled the morphine, and from that day forward the elbow therapy was accomplished without drugs.

Oh, the physical pain was still present, but in its place were renewed feelings of self-respect and dignity. The knowledge that I had met another challenge on my journey made me feel good about myself. In my mind, I walked a bit taller from that day forward.

Over the next few weeks, the range of motion in my elbow gradually increased and permitted me the chance to eat my Thanksgiving dinner without assistance. The turkey and all the trimmings seemed to have an extra special taste.

The dynamic splint remained on my arm for more than two months after surgery.

I spent the remaining four weeks waiting for my first convalescent leave which was scheduled for Christmas, 1970. Even though many more surgeries were planned, they would wait until after Christmas.

My daily routine, though monotonous at times, was never boring. Being able to feed myself had just taken on a whole new meaning, and I greeted every meal like it was my first.

Wake up, eat breakfast, attend physical therapy, sleep, watch television, read, visit with the other patients and staff, see my wife, and mentally prepare for more surgeries. Twice a month the Red Cross treated us to a fashion show with cookies and punch. Other than family, the Red Cross volunteers were the only visitors to the burn ward. The cookies and punch were good, and visits by females other than our spouses were a positive diversion and helped keep us energized.

My physical being continued to feel stronger every day!

One afternoon in early December 1970, I visited again with Dr. Inge in the nurse's break room located next to the ICU. My reason for wanting to talk to him focused on my future and our planned visit home for the first time since the plane crash.

I had another, even more important reason for wanting to talk to him. Over the previous several weeks, two of my ICU nurses, Captains Sheri McGhee and Myra Peche, told me about the time and energy Dr. Inge spent working on me during my eighty-nine-day stay in the ICU. What they told me was hard to fathom and confirming their stories became important to me.

Dr. Inge, like the other burn doctors, had other patients besides me for whom he was responsible, making the time he spent with me even more important. Given his busy schedule, he was under no obligation to sit down and talk with me as often as he did.

As soon as he entered the break room, I started peppering him with questions.

"Sheri and Myra told me that several times during my eighty-nine days in the ICU, you never left the unit and most of that time was spent working on me. They told me you stayed here and didn't go home. Is this true?"

"Why George, what difference would it make if I said yes?" he asked.

"I need to know," I said and asked him again.

"Did you work on me several times twenty-four hours in a row without stopping?"

He appeared quite reluctant to respond, looked at the ceiling, then his eyes returned to me.

"Yes, I did George," he replied.

"Why did you do that?"

Once again, he paused, his eyes looking at the ceiling, then he looked directly at me.

"You know, George," he said, "we lose a lot of patients here. There was something about you which made me even more determined to do everything in my power to try and help you get better."

"Well, I'm really glad you did," I responded, "and I can't begin to tell you my feelings of gratitude." Saying thank you to him seemed so shallow and insufficient.

"You're welcome George," he replied. "You know George," he continued, "we need a George Burk to come through here every so often to justify to all of us that what we do makes a difference in some peoples' lives; it helps keep all of our morale high."

"Did you ever sleep during this time?" I asked.

"Yes," he said, "in the nurse's locker room just down the hall on an Army cot."

"Hmm," I thought, "Sheri and Myra were right."

After our meeting, I made it my singular mission to verify a cot was in the nurses' locker room. It was!

My questions then shifted to his spiritual beliefs, and I shared with him my two near-death-experiences.

"Why," I asked, "did I come back while the others on the boat continued to cross the bridge, through the door and into the bright light?"

"I don't know George," he said. "Perhaps the Lord had a reason for you not dying at that particular time. Perhaps He has a plan for you. You will just have to be patient and await the outcome. It probably will not come all at once or when you would most expect it or want it to happen," he said.

"The plan may be something that occurs over the rest of your life. It is up to you to find that purpose, no one can do it for you."

Dr. Inge continued explaining how he and the staff realized my willingness to fight. My long struggle in the ICU and my family's support made me special in their eyes. My sense of humor throughout my many illnesses picked up those around me and helped them feel better about what they were trying to accomplish.

"Well, what am I supposed to do now with my second chance at life?" I asked.

"Maybe after your release from here," he said, "you can use what you have experienced as a positive and pass your experiences about burns and fire prevention to others. If you can prevent one more person from becoming a statistic, then our tasks and your extended stay here would have meant something. One less patient right now we could really use."

Dr. Inge believed that time and my re-entry into society would help me discover a renewed purpose in my life. He also suggested that sharing my story with others could have a number of positive effects not only on the audience but for me.

One benefit he suggested is that people might be more careful in their daily lives, follow safe procedures, and use protective equipment while handling toxic and flammable liquids. Talking to others about my injuries might also act as an emotional outlet and release for me and help others find the motivation to overcome adversity.

Over the years since my release from the hospital, I've had the opportunity to address different groups about safety, fire prevention, overcoming adversity, setting and achieving goals and finding a purpose in life. The positive feedback I have received has enhanced the quality of my life.

Then I told him in vivid detail my two "out-of-body experiences." The first, walking across the bridge with Colonel Shelton, looking up, seeing a door, the smell of flowers and a bright light. The second, looking down a long tunnel, seeing two silhouettes outlined in front of a bright light. Then, a loud rush of wind, and standing in front of me were Ken Yarger and Fred Adams.

After listening to me detail these two events, Dr. Inge crossed his arms over his chest, leaned back in the chair and looked at the ceiling.

"Now I know what you were trying to tell us," he said.

"Tell you what?" I asked.

"One day," he continued, "we were working on you trying to get you to respond."

"Suddenly, you opened your eyes and started yelling," he continued.

"What was I yelling?" I asked.

"'The light! the light!'" you yelled over and over again.

"'What light, George, what light?'" we asked.

"'The light! the light!'" you screamed. Your voice kept getting higher and higher and you became more agitated."

"Well," he said, "We thought it was the lights around your bed were hurting your eyes and we moved them, thinking that was what you were trying to tell us."

"Your agitation and shaking increased," he said, "so I sedated you so you would stop screaming and go back to sleep."

"It was a pretty anxious time for us," he said.

"Me too...I guess," I responded.

Then I knew that what I had experienced was real. It has stayed with me all these years and continues to be my source of prayer, inspiration and faith.

Our conversation then shifted to my release from the hospital.

"How long do you think it will be before I get out of here?" I asked.

"That is up to you George," he replied, "and other factors over which we have little control. Knowing and seeing how fast you have responded thus far, if I had to estimate today, I'd say you might be released within the next twelve months."

"Wow!" I exclaimed, "You don't know how that sounds to me. It's music to my burned ears."

Without knowing it, I had made a "funny" and we both laughed. Yet, twelve months seemed like a long, long time. We spent the remaining time that day discussing the planned surgeries on my hand, face and stub. With nothing else to discuss, Dr. Inge excused himself to begin afternoon rounds.

"What time is it Doc?" I asked.

"Ten o'clock," he said.

We chuckled. Our meeting had lasted longer than two hours and my legs, buttocks and back felt it too!

I got up slowly from the chair and thanked him again for taking time to visit with me and for all he had done to save my life. I walked out the door, down the marble hallway past several offices and waited for the elevator. As I exited the elevator, my thoughts drifted to how far I had come in the past few months, how much more work remained, and appreciation for Dr. Inge and the staff's commitment to me and to my family.

My thoughts were temporarily distracted when a nurse greeted me by name as I shuffled past the nurses' station. As I walked into the ward, I was greeted by catcalls from several of the guys who weren't sleeping.

"Hey Captain, where in the hell have you been? It's about time you got back," several shouted. "We were beginning to worry about you," they said laughing.

"Yeah, right," I said. "The only thing you guys worry about is your next meal, getting an erection and taking a leak by yourself."

Before realizing it, I was standing next to my bed. The past few minutes were a blur. I couldn't remember getting on the elevator nor walking down the hallway after visiting with Dr. Inge. The time simply vanished.

"Nothing wrong with my mind," I thought. " I'm tired, my legs are bothering me and I want to sleep," I mumbled and climbed into the safety and security of my bed.

As I started to doze off, many of the experiences since arriving at the hospital raced through my mind like a movie on fast forward. I replayed the events which, while horrible and painful to recall, were such an important part of my physical and mental journey.

I recall being lifted carefully from my bed and placed on a gurney, transferred to a cart with a white sheet and prepared for the stressful ride to the back of the ward for debridement. A feeling of absolute terror and helplessness overcame me as I was lowered into one of the white, stainless steel tanks where the corpsmen and nurses prepared to remove the dead skin using scalpels, files and razor blades. I begged Dr. Inge and the nurses to leave me alone.

I pleaded, "Don't do that to me, please!"

The cold and sterile physical surroundings of the tanking rooms heightened my awareness of what was going to happen. Nothing in my life, to that point or since, has duplicated the fear and helplessness felt each time the staff debrided the skin.

Being skinned alive is the worst kind of physical pain imaginable and it scared the absolute hell out of all of us. We dreaded this procedure more than any of the other types of treatment. It made grown men cry, beg for mercy and plead to be left alone. It was a feeling of being violated...violating me as a human being...slicing and digging my skin off my body!

Reaching the tank room, the corpsmen removed the white sheet from my body and the coldness immediately increased. My mind was alert to the pending pain and discomfort. Lowered into the tank by the two corpsmen, the warm saline solution enveloped me like a soothing, warm blanket. All the while my anxiety continued to build. My feeling of security quickly faded when I heard the tinny, metal sound of scalpels, razors and other similar devices placed on the small table next to the tank. Immersed up to my chest in the warm water, with both arms dangling at my side and floating in the water, the corpsmen and nurses began cutting away dead skin.

On one occasion, I remember looking up to my right and seeing Myra Peche leaning over the right side of the tank. A white gauze mask covered her mouth and nose, a bonnet covered her head, and she was squeezing a black bulb attached to my throat. The black bulb was helping me breathe.

Another time while being "tanked," I remember seeing a walkway attached to the opposite wall from the tank and people were standing on the platform watching me. Above the walkway hung a number of colorful pennants attached to the wall, and in the background the sound of helicopter blades cutting through the air, "whup, whup, whup," startled me.

Several months later, after my visits to the tank rooms were complete, I returned to both rooms to confirm the existence of a walkway and pennants. As I walked into one of the rooms, I saw one of our nurses cleaning out the tank.

"Hey," I asked, "what happened to the pennants and the walkway in here?"

"What?" she asked.

"What happened to the pennants and walkway in here?" I asked again.

"There have never been any pennants or a walkway in this room or the other room."

"Are you sure?" I asked.

"No pennants, no walkway. The morphine and your sub-conscious mind must have really been playing tricks with you," she said.

"Yeah, I guess so," I replied. "Guess my mind was trying to compensate for the pain any way it could."

She nodded in agreement, and we both walked into the corridor and returned to the main part of the ward.

During the eighty-nine days in the ICU, my 'dreams' never had me in a hospital, but always someplace away from the hospital. My mind was trying to ease my pain and, in all actuality, preparing to die. In one scene, I am lying on the living room floor of our base house at Hamilton Air Force Base.

"Here comes Bobby Ward again," I yelled. "Bobby, don't slam the screen door."

Then the scene shifts to work where we are all seated at our respective desks, talking about a scheduled inspection trip, Vietnam or another "hot" topic of the day. The faces and names are always the same. Billy Bishop, Fred

Adams, Kenny Yarger and the other non-commissioned officers in the office with whom I worked.

The one constant in all the dreams is the feeling of being sick and cold and knowing something was wrong but lacking the physical strength to lift my head or get up and look around.

"Why can't someone help me and make the pain and discomfort go away?" I screamed to myself over and over again then would fall into a listless sleep. The dreams continued in a replay of specific events of my life.

I saw scenes of lying in the tank while a corpsmen and nurse were preparing to debride my skin. Sheri McGhee leaned over from the right side of the tank and tried to comfort me.

"Please leave me alone," I begged. "It hurts, damn it!" I yelled.

"Turn over, George," Dr. Inge yelled in a stern voice.

"Leave me alone. I'm not rolling over," I yelled back. "It's too hard, and I don't feel good."

"Roll over, George," he yelled at me again.

"I'm not rolling over for you, leave me alone, it hurts!" I yelled. Silence. He knew I heard and understood him, but I was just being obstinate.

"C'mon you fat son-of-a-bitch, roll over!" he yelled a third time.

"No one is going to call me a fat son-of-a-bitch and get away with it," I thought. I rolled over on my left side. His calling me a "fat son-of-a-bitch" really made me mad.

Later on, the nurses told me that Dr. Inge would repeatedly thrust a scalpel into my thigh to provoke me to respond to his urging…proving I still had the will to live.

The burning pain from the newly grafted skin on my lower back being cut and scraped away pulsed through my brain. My cries to be left alone were being ignored. However, unknown to me at the time, Dr. Inge was literally saving my life again.

As my family related to me months later, Dr. Inge came to them during this time and said he was afraid I was quitting and giving up. He needed to find a way to get me to respond.

My medical signs all pointed to another serious, life-threatening infection, and he finally determined it must be under the newly grafted skin on my lower back. Dr. Inge told my family that he was unable to get me to respond to his commands and roll over on my side in the tank to cut out the infected tissue.

"Is there anything about George that makes him mad?" he asked my wife.

"Well," she said, "he's really conscious about his weight."

"What about his weight?" he asked.

"Well," she continued, "if he gains just a few pounds over the weekend, he works out extra hard the next week to lose the weight he gained."

"Good," he replied. "I'll try that and see what happens."

Needless to say, his efforts worked.

On another occasion, when another series of infections in my arms and legs threatened my life, the other doctors and consultants were asked for their advice. To a person, the response was unanimous.

"Take the hands, take the arms, take the legs," they suggested.

Again, he waited to talk to my family and asked them what they wanted him to do.

"What do you want me to do?" he asked.

"Save whatever you can," was their reply.

Today, I am able to enjoy life using both of my arms and both legs. God's love, Dr. Inge's relentless commitment and caring attitude, and my family's love and support are the reasons I am alive today.

In December 1970, eight months after the crash, I had a number of reconstructive surgeries yet to endure, but Dr. Inge approved my thirty-day convalescent leave. He said my recovery since leaving the ICU was so rapid that time away from the hospital would give me more emotional benefit than remaining in the hospital. The collective medical wisdom believed my next plateau towards the recovery process was now psychological instead of purely physical, although there is a direct correlation between the two.

It was time for me to go home, regroup emotionally, relax, visit my family and get away from the stress of the burn unit.

Our scheduled itinerary had us flying to Detroit and spending seven days with my in-laws, then to Pittsburgh to visit my parents and family. The weeks leading up to our flight to Detroit were filled with great trepidation for me.

The trip was my first flight on an airplane since the plane crash, and I had many sleepless nights reliving the plane decompression after takeoff. Several nights before our departure, I awoke from a deep sleep drenched in perspiration after reliving the plane crash. In my dreams, I'm seated in the same seat, preparing to take a nap, then, "boom," the plane explodes, blowing out the windows, and we begin our tortuous descent. On our ride down, the tree branches brush over and under the wings, slide underneath out of sight and shower the air with broken limbs and leaves.

The scent of eucalyptus trees is always present as the limbs and leaves fly past the open windows. Just before impact, wet in my own sweat, my dream is interrupted. This dream is still part of my life, and I experience it several times a year with the same results. I survive.

Climbing aboard another airplane was not the most important thing in my life at that time. But my fear of getting back on a plane was exceeded by my desire to go home. I knew that I couldn't live in a glass house and was determined that the fear of flying would not overtake and control my life.

"Do the thing you fear the most and the death of fear is certain," is the quote that played over and over again inside my head.

Our trip home would also provide another "why" in my life and I already knew I could endure almost any "how."

Our day of departure finally arrived. We arrived at the airport early to ensure I had enough time to walk to the gate. I refused to have anyone transport me in a cart. We arrived at the gate with time to spare and made ready to board the plane. A flight attendant assisted me to my seat and made sure my seat belt was properly attached.

"Can I get you something to drink before we take off?" she asked.

"Yes Ma'am," I said. "A shot of Irish whiskey."

I laughed and told her it was only a joke. My scarring was obvious, and I think she sensed my trepidation.

At that time, the conflict in Vietnam was still ongoing and she probably thought I was injured on active duty. I often wondered what she would have said or done had I told her that this flight was my first since being the sole survivor of a plane crash. Our flight to Detroit was uneventful and actually kind of fun for me. Hooo-ah!

During the three-and-one-half hour flight, my thoughts were on family and home. Mom's cooking, Aunt Anne's special cakes, a cold Iron City beer, fish sandwiches, the special smells of our home and the schoolyard where I played many games of basketball and stick-ball.

Then, I was startled awake by the flight attendant announcing our arrival in Detroit and urging us to make sure our seat belts were fastened. She didn't have to tell me!

Chapter Fourteen: Home For The Holidays

"Effort fully releases its reward only after a person refuses to quit."
                                          Napoleon Hill

On December 20th, after a week in Michigan, we drove to Pittsburgh, Pennsylvania. We arrived in the early afternoon.

As we approached the far northwestern city limits, I had a sense of familiarity that signaled I was really going home. With every passing second, my anticipation continued to build.

"How fast are you going?" I asked Nancy. "Can't you hurry up?" I begged like a child.

We drove through the narrow paved streets of the Pittsburgh suburbs. Every minute took us closer to Sheraden, the community where I was born and raised, three and one-half miles from downtown Pittsburgh. Through Corliss Tunnel, over the bridge which crosses over the train tracks, turning right past the bakeries, grocery stores, Dietrick's Tavern, the post office and up the hill.

"Only a minute or two from home now," I thought. "Wonder if Mom will be standing on the front porch."

Through my flannel shirt and winter coat I could feel my heart pulse in my chest and in my neck. For some strange reason, the streets seemed narrower than I remembered.

We turned left at the top of the hill, then right on Hammond Street, and Harwood School and the schoolyard quickly appeared on our left. Harwood Elementary School, where four generations of my family attended school, standing there in all its splendor like an old temple of knowledge.

"There's the house, and I can see Mom standing on the porch," I said.

As soon as she recognized the car, I saw Mom dart back into the house—probably to tell Dad that we had arrived.

We turned left at the corner, past the small yard and wrought iron fence which bordered my old church, the Sheraden United Methodist, then came to a stop in front of the house, just past Mueller's Bakery.

"I'm home, I made it," I thought. "Another milestone in my recovery. " I took a deep breath, opened the car door and slowly got out of the car.

When I stood up and glanced towards the house, I saw Mom peering through the living room curtains. Then the front door flew open and down the steps to the sidewalk she raced and grabbed and hugged me so tight I couldn't breathe.

"Mom, be careful," I pleaded. "I didn't survive the plane crash to be crushed by you."

"Oh," she said, "I'm sorry honey. We're just so glad you are home!"

As Mom helped me up the steps, we stopped briefly to say hello to our neighbors, Mr. and Mrs. Deitz and their daughter Janie, standing in their front yard waiting for our arrival. Then we walked into the house.

As I walked into the hallway, I noticed the house had retained all its character; the smell, stairs, carpet, furniture, everything just as I pictured it would be hundreds of times in the hospital. After Mom removed my coat, leggings and boots, I realized how exhausted I was from the trip and made a beeline to my favorite green recliner.

As soon as I sat down in the recliner, Mom started hovering over me, telling me what there was to eat and making certain that I was warm and comfortable.

"Mom," I said, "if I need anything, I will let you know. I just want to sit here and relax."

I loved every minute of her attention.

A few hours after arriving, I set out to accomplish one of the goals I set for myself, dreaming of this moment while in the hospital. I lowered the recliner's handle and stood up, careful not to lose my balance and walked slowly to the foot of the stairs.

"Where are you going?" Mom yelled, standing in front of the stove.

"Upstairs," I said.

"Oh, no you're not," she said.

George's mother, Willa Burk, 1984

"You're not going up those stairs. What happens if you fall?" she asked.

"Mom," I replied, "I won't fall; I'll be careful. This is another thing I've been thinking about for a long time."

Negotiating my way up the stairs, I began recalling the times I walked these stairs as a younger man. Going to baseball and basketball games, leaving on dates, waking up the morning after our championship game when I was a high school junior.

"Hmm," I thought, stopping at the top of the stairs, "I want to go up in the attic where I slept and dig through all those old pictures."

George Burk at 15.

"George," Mom yelled up from the foot of the stairs, "are you all right?"

"Yes, Mom," I replied.

"Dinner is almost ready," she said. "Take your time on the stairs, but come back down here now."

"Okay, I'm coming back down now," I said.

Walking was still a challenge, especially when ascending and descending stairs. When I reached the first floor, I walked to the rear of the house to find Mom and see what she was cooking for dinner.

The aroma of turkey and ham cooking in the oven smelled wonderful and made me salivate. My stomach was growling; dinner was an eagerly awaited event.

"I'm going down to the cellar," I said.

"Oh, no you're not," Mom exclaimed. "You might fall down the cellar steps and reinjure yourself."

"If I fall, I fall," I answered and walked to the cellar door and opened it.

Carefully, one slow step after another, I negotiated my way down the old wooden steps. Each one creaked under my feet. I reached the foot of the steps, turned right and walked to the small shower where I used to shower after baseball games. The smell of that old cellar and seeing the shower head attached to the wall underneath the cellar steps brought back even more pleasant memories. The thousands of showers after playing baseball games and drinking a large, plastic container of orange juice.

"You're not dreaming," I thought. "This is real. It feels good to be home."

After spending several minutes reflecting on my younger days in that house, my thoughts were interrupted by Mom's exhortations to come back upstairs.

"George, come up for dinner and be careful walking up the steps," she said.

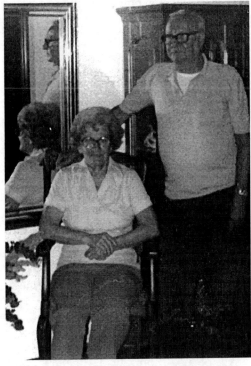

George Burk's parents, Willa and Walter Burk, 1978

"Okay, Mom," I replied, "I'm on my way now."

When I reached the top step, I heard the familiar sound of the front door bell ringing and the voice of my cousin, Tom Parrish, echoed throughout the house. I have always thought of Tom and his brother, Bud, as being like older brothers.

"Where is he? Where is George?" Tom yelled, walking down the hallway.

As I reached the top step and turned to my left, Tom entered the kitchen. As our eyes met, Tom stopped and looked at me, then embraced me in a bear hug.

"You're all right," he said. "You made it," and started to cry.

We stood there hugging each other for several minutes and two men couldn't have hugged each other longer or hard enough. Tom squeezed me so hard, I had difficulty breathing.

"Yes!" I thought. "Another bridge crossed on my road to recovery."

Tom's response made me feel better about myself and helped erase my doubts about my family accepting me as a burn survivor. Tom stayed for two hours and when he left, he promised to return the next day with Miriam and their children.

The next few days were hectic. Time was spent visiting with Aunt Anne Parrish, uncles, aunts and cousins. It was all a blur of talk, food and the enjoyment of sharing quality time with my family.

All of us, Mom, Dad, Nancy, Aunt Anne and my children, Walter, Kimberly, and Scott, attended church our first Sunday at home.

The small Sheraden Terrace United Methodist Church was our family's church, a short two-minute walk around the corner from home. I was baptized there and attended Sunday school and church from kindergarten through high school. Even though it was close to home, I attended inconsistently, especially during my teen years, when sleeping late on a Sunday seemed more important than visiting with the Lord.

George Burk with his father, Walter, 1957

Interesting, isn't it—how significant emotional events can play such an important role in a person's life.

That Sunday at church was special! Unknown to me, the pastor had planned with my mother that I should share my accident, rescue, recovery, and my two near-death experiences with the congregation. During the service, I was invited to the pulpit to speak.

The church was crowded that Sunday. Many had heard of my trials and were there in anticipation of seeing me again and hearing about the crash and my rescue.

Some might think it would be hard to stand before a crowd and reveal details of something so intensely personal, but as I shared with the congregation, I was so moved by their response that the story seemed to flow like a well-rehearsed script, something I was intended to deliver. I was eager to share how the crash had such a positive influence on me, my family and my hopes and my dreams. I recounted my attempts to recall the small things in life I used to take for granted and how much more vivid and important the little things in life had become: the smell of the air after a fresh rain, freshly cut grass, and the sound and feel of snow crunching under foot. The burns, illnesses and emotional trauma had erased those smells and sounds so that every experience of life was new to me—like learning to walk again.

Sharing my two near-death experiences and the belief that GOD saved my life for a purpose was the highlight of my talk and seemed to uplift everyone in the church.

My talk at the church was an emotional, yet comforting and stimulating experience for me. It was the best emotional therapy I could receive. I closed my remarks by thanking everyone there for their prayers and cards for me and my family.

Later that afternoon, after taking my usual nap, I stood in the living room and looked out to see falling snow cover cars, trees and the street in a blanket of white.

Once again, the flashbacks raced through my mind. While I was in the hospital I had tried with all my energy to remember the look, sound and smell of snow. Now, with the snow falling outside, those memories were slowly returning.

"I'm actually standing here in my home looking at all this," I thought.

Standing there in the living room and watching snow falling outside, the smell of dinner cooking in the kitchen and the laughter of my family overwhelmed me.

"I'm glad I didn't quit and give up," I thought. "Just think what I would have missed."

I pinched myself on the left arm to make sure I was not dreaming.

"Thank you, God," I said. "Thank you, Dr. Inge. Thanks, Fred, Kenny, Colonel Shelton."

"Hey, everybody," I yelled. "It's really snowing and looks like it is sticking, and I'm going for a walk."

My wish had come true!

After convincing my family I would not freeze and blow away, Mom, Billie Ann and Nancy helped me put on thermal socks, leggings and insulated boots and buttoned the heavy flannel shirt and insulated jacket.

Next was the prescription cream for my face, then a face mask, and a heavy woolen cap for my head. Heavy gloves and mittens underneath the gloves were next, then coveralls over the leggings. I looked like The Pillsbury Doughboy!

I waddled like a duck out the front door and with Mom, Nancy, and Billie Ann supporting me under my arms so I wouldn't fall, we stepped onto the front porch and down the steps to the sidewalk.

We turned left and walked the fifty yards or so to the corner, turned left again and walked up the street, past the church to Aunt Anne's house. A walk I had taken hundreds of times before, but this time my anticipation of seeing her again and just being able to walk made this walk extra special.

As we walked on the snow-covered sidewalk, the snow swirled around us, and we could see our breath in the cold December early evening. The street lights glowed with snow swirling around the lights and sticking to the telephone poles. The sound of snow crunching under my feet was like music to my ears. But my elation quickly turned to tears as I remembered lying in the hospital trying to recall the sound snow made as it crunched under foot. My tears of joy froze on my eyelashes and my emotion was contagious. My helpers were crying too.

Reaching Aunt Anne's house, we stopped at the front steps and waited to see if she would appear at the door.

"Aunt Anne, c'mon out," I hollered.

I looked at the living room window and saw the curtains move and waited. Suddenly, the front door flew open and Aunt Anne walked quickly out onto the front porch and met me at the top of the steps. She grabbed me and gave me a big hug and kiss.

"Welcome home, honey," she said.

"Thanks, Aunt Anne," I said.

"I'm glad you made it back. I love you."

We stood there enjoying the moment and talked about how I was feeling, what it was like being home, and my plans for tomorrow. The weather was getting colder, and I wanted to get back home. We walked around the block and returned home.

Through this whole adventure, my family was fearful I'd either fall and reinjure myself or the cold would make me sick and hasten my return to the hospital. Their concerns were not totally misplaced, but a walk in the snow was something I had to do. I had come this far, a little snow wasn't going to stop me. God, Life, I love you!

Two days later, December 23, 1970, all of the family who lived in Pittsburgh gathered at Aunt Anne's house for a special Christmas dinner and family reunion. The food was plentiful and delicious. There was ham, turkey, chicken, steak, three kinds of potatoes, stuffing and the usual wonderful desserts. As the family's guest of honor, I was seated at the head of the table with my wife, my Mom, Dad, Aunt Anne and Uncle Otto Parrish.

As part of my family's custom, a great deal of bantering and good-natured kidding was also on the menu. As more Iron City beer and wine were consumed, the good-natured kidding intensified. Looking over my family from the head of the table, I had a sense of great progress, yet was aware of the surgeries which awaited me when I would return to the hospital.

"Stop," I thought, "don't think. This is a time for me to enjoy my family and eat. Boy, I'm glad to be here! Damn, Dr. Inge knew what he was talking about again."

Being home with my family was the perfect antidote to possible discouragement, and I felt myself getting stronger and stronger with every passing minute.

Being near my family and away from the hospital re-energized my mental and physical batteries for the balance of my journey. The visit home was a critical stage in my emotional and physical recovery. Even today, I think of this period of time as the beginning of my transition from being a victim of tragedy to becoming a triumphant survivor.

We celebrated Christmas, and I enjoyed visiting with a number of former high school classmates who stopped by to say hello and wish me well. It had been a hectic but enjoyable two weeks at home. The sooner I returned to the hospital, the quicker the surgeries would end and my release from the hospital would come closer to reality.

My once-distant vision of seeing myself walk out of the hospital under my own power was approaching realization and I began mentally preparing myself for what was ahead.

On January 3, 1971, we returned to the farm southeast of Hudson, Michigan, and stayed there for three days. On January 6, my in-lawsdrove us to the Detroit Metropolitan Airport for the non-stop flight to San Antonio. I already missed my family, but I missed my hospital family too. All the doctors, nurses, corpsmen and the other guys on the ward. They were part of my family now and forever in my heart. I still felt safer on the burn ward, absent the stares and furtive glances of people who had never before seen a burn survivor.

From January 1971 to September 1971, eight surgical procedures on my hands and two experimental surgeries on my face and neck were completed. During the surgeries on my left stub, the orthopedic surgeons, assisted by Dr. Inge, removed the index-finger, ring-finger and little-finger bones from the stub and created a cleft.

After the grafting healed, physical therapy was initiated, and I was to learn how to grab or pinch small objects with the cleft. It didn't work very well.

Four years later, in the Spring of 1975, I returned to the hospital where surgery was performed to enhance the cleft's functionality. The doctors broke the knuckles of my third and fourth metacarpal bones, then inserted a "k" wire in each bone. The surgical procedure involved the doctors breaking the metacarpal bones and the thumb knuckle with a high speed drill, then bending each bone slightly forward. The "k" wires were to hold everything in the right orientation while the bones knit. Two months after the surgery, the wires were removed. It was hoped the procedure would increase the functionality of my cleft by ten percent so I could grasp items like a money clip and tie my shoe laces and ties. The operation was successful.

Slowly, my stay in the warm comfort of the burn unit was coming to an end. During the latter part of 1970, I talked with Dr. Inge, my family and my military supervisors at Richards-Gebaur Air Force Base, Missouri, about remaining on active duty. Certain my returning to active duty in the Air Force was a long shot, it was still in my best interests to explore all options.

The Headquarters Commander at Hamilton at the time of the crash, Colonel Jim Neff, his wife "Fletch" and their daughters Jeannie and Jane visited me at the hospital and kept in touch through my family. He and General Paul Stoney, our Commanding General, had received daily status briefings on my condition throughout my eighteen months in the hospital.

Chapter Fifteen: You're Outta Here!

"The bend in the road is not the end of the road unless you fail to make the turn."   *Anonymous*

In September, 1970, during an official visit to Randolph Air Force Base near San Antonio, General Stoney arranged to stop and visit me. The day of his visit was an exciting yet hectic time for everyone involved.

In preparation for his visit, my hair, or what remained of it, was washed and combed by a nurse. Then she dressed me in clean blue hospital pajamas, helped me back into bed, and I anxiously awaited his arrival.

Knowing General Stoney was making a special trip to see me increased my nervousness, and I hoped my appearance would not be too disturbing to him or his entourage.

The morning of his arrival, the sky was thick with fog and a light rain was falling. Looking out the windows from my hospital bed, the fog looked like a large, gray blanket. General Stoney was scheduled to arrive at eight o'clock in the morning but was delayed due to the weather. Shortly after eight o'clock, I began asking anyone nearby the time.

"Hey, what time is it?" I'd ask.

"Eight-fifteen," then "Eight-thirty, " was the reply.

"He isn't coming," I thought. "Of all days, why does it have to be foggy today?"

In the hope that somehow my shuffling from my bed to the windows on the porch would speed his arrival, I asked a nurse to help me out of bed. I walked over to the porch and looked out of the windows.

Suddenly, while trying to manage my nervousness about his arrival, I heard a corpsmen make an announcement at the entrance to the ward.

"He's here," he said.

"The General is here," he repeated. "He's coming up the elevator now and will be here in a minute."

I was relieved he had finally arrived, and I asked a nurse to check my hair, make certain the large gauze wrap around my left stub was clean and taped, and that my pajama buttons were buttoned.

"Hey," she said, "you look great."

"Yeah, right," I said sarcastically.

Before I realized it, General Stoney walked into the ward, and was standing in front of me. His aide and staff members stood behind and to his right. General Stoney greeted me warmly and expressed all command's "warmest best wishes."

"General," I said, "I caution you about using words like 'warmest' on a burn ward."

"Gotcha, General, "I said smiling. My comment broke the tension.

His look of embarrassment changed quickly to laughter.

I didn't know General Stoney was also there to present me the Air Force Commendation Medal. He was handed the medal from his aide and proceeded to pin the medal on my pajama top, just above the left breast pocket.

The General was a man about five-foot seven inches tall but much taller in professional stature. Even as I bent forward slightly, I was about five inches taller than he.

"George," he said, "I don't remember you being this tall. I wish I had several of your inches."

"That makes us even General," I replied, "I wish I had one of your stars."

We both laughed at my feeble attempt at humor.

"Well, you never know what may happen," he said.

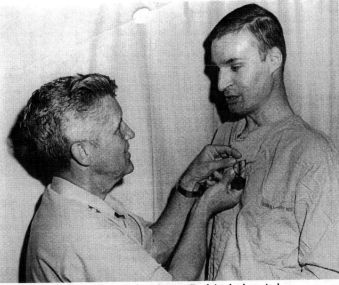

General Stoney pins the medal on George Burk in the hospital.

"George," he continued, "I want you to know that, in or out of the service, you have a position on my staff." His comments really energized me.

"Just what the doctor ordered," I thought. "Knowing I have a job when I leave here will help me endure all the stuff yet to come. "

General Stoney's comment gave me yet another "why" in my life and I knew that enduring almost any "how" was a bit easier now, knowing my job prospects were not as bleak as I'd envisioned.

My professional goal to become a General Officer was not to be realized. In late October, 1971, the Physical

Evaluation Board (PEB) met at Randolph Air Force Base to review my medical records and determine my fitness for active duty. The Board's findings were unanimous. I was unable to perform my military duties and, because of the burns and internal injuries, could not be cleared for world-wide duty.

The process to medically retire me from the Air Force was initiated.

However, all the news was not negative. General Stoney kept his pledge, and I was hired as a civilian employee on the Air Traffic Control staff at the Headquarters, Richards-Gebaur Air Force Base, Missouri, and worked there for seven years. As my life was resuming, I thought of my friends who had not made it through with me.

During my employment at Richards-Gebaur, I had the opportunity to get to know and work with many dedicated people. Some of them, in addition to Colonel Neff and General Stoney, were Colonel Bill Wilson, Charlie Antweiler, Paul Herriott, Pete Young, Al Gray, Phil Walker, John Edstrom, Ward Baker, John Spears, Ron Jones, Charlene (Chuck) Culver, Gabe Hartl, Rich Flack, Harvey Greer, Ward Seiler, and Jane Schroer.

There have been many others. The fog of time has clouded their names from my mind, but I still cherish grateful memories of their efforts on my behalf and how they helped me. They made me feel welcome and grateful I had survived. I am a fortunate man to have had the opportunity and privilege of meeting and working with men and women who took great personal and professional pride in themselves. Any success I achieved in my life is due, in part, to their patience and understanding.

Chapter Sixteen: ATΩ Class Ring

"Everywhere I go, there I am again."　　　　　*Pogo*

I graduated from Adrian College, Adrian, Michigan, in 1963. Like many college graduates, I received my college class ring as a gift from my parents.

Knowing that Mom and Dad really couldn't afford the cost of the ring made me appreciate it even more, especially later in my life. The ring has a large ruby stone in honor of my July birthday and my Greek fraternity symbols "ATΩ" engraved in the center of the stone. Inside the ring's band are my initials, "GAB", in script. I seldom went a day without wearing my ring on my right ring finger.

Perhaps during my rescue, while I was in the emergency room at Hamilton AFB or enroute to the burn unit in San Antonio on board the Air Force C141 Starlifter, someone removed my ring.

After all, my hands were burned black and swollen. Worrying about my class ring was the last thing on my mind. I had far more important issues to occupy my time and thoughts.

For twenty-seven years after the crash, I forgot about my class ring. The few times I would think about it, I dismissed the thought just as rapidly. Like my watch and other personal belongings, I believed my ring was lost in the crash and held no hope of ever seeing it again.

Then, on March 8, 1998, twenty-eight years after the crash, the story of my lost class ring took a bizarre turn. I received an e-mail message from Ms. Colleen Kowich, a volunteer in the Adrian College Alumni Office. Colleen's message was, "George, this e-mail message sounds like it may be good news. Let me know. I checked all our records for the year 1963 and your name is the only one with the initials GAB."

At the end of Colleen's message was a second message from Mr. Charles Carrington of Sacramento, California.

His e-mail to Colleen read, "I found a class ring in the military awhile back. The initials are GAB in script and the year is 1963. If you have someone who lost their ring while at Charleston AFB, SC, have them e-mail me. Thanks."

On March 9th, I e-mailed Charles Carrington, identified myself as the potential owner of the ring and provided my home address and phone number. I also asked Charles to either call or e-mail me at his earliest convenience as I had a lot of questions about how he found the ring. On March 10th, Charles returned my e-mail and provided me the following details. He found the ring at the officer's club restroom during a stop over on his way to Germany to participate in a Crested Cap NATO exercise. At the time, he was assigned to the 49th Tactical Fighter Wing, Holloman AFB, New Mexico, and was a Weapons Systems Officer (WSO) flying the F4D Phantom Fighter/Bomber aircraft.

On Sunday evening, March 15, 1998, at six o'clock, Charles called me at home. We visited for ten minutes and I provided him my home address. Charles told me the ring would be on its way and I should have it in a few days. During our conversation, Charles said he found the ring in a small soap dish above one of the sinks in the officer's club men's room in late 1970 or early 1971. He couldn't remember the exact date.

Charles picked up the ring, commented to himself on its nice appearance and thought it a bit strange someone would leave his class ring there, then placed it in his flight suit.

He departed later that evening for Germany, lost track of the ring and recently discovered it in his personal belongings packed away since his Air Force retirement. His discovery of the ring led him to locate the college on the Internet and contact the alumni office.

My family and I are certain I was wearing the ring the morning of the plane crash in the hills near Napa, California. How the ring made its way nearly 3,000 miles from Northern California across the country to Charleston, AFB, South Carolina, can only be left to speculation and conjecture.

Perhaps the Air Force C-141 Starlifter and its flight crew who transported me to the burn unit in San Antonio were stationed at Charleston AFB. Perhaps the Air Force flight nurse removed my ring from my right hand, planned to return it to me, misplaced the ring, then simply forgot about it. Nurses, like many others in the military in those days, were quite busy serving in Vietnam and caring for the men and women injured in battle and in plane crashes.

Perhaps someone who found the ring removed it to wash his hands and forgot where he placed it. Literally, a few minutes afterwards, Charles Carrington found the ring lying in the dish above a wash basin in the men's room.

Why then? Why that wash basin? Why Charles Carrington? If someone else had found the ring, would the outcome have been the same? So many questions and so few real answers. Perhaps the story of how my college class ring made its way across the country will never be known.

Like the reasons I was "accidentally" discovered by John Davieau and the many other factors which led to my rescue, the story will never be fully known. Only God knows.

Maybe I'm not supposed to know, but am supposed to accept what has happened and continue to move my life forward. I am convinced there are still positive forces working in my life.

On May 2, 2002, I had the opportunity to finally meet Charles Carrington, the man who found my ring. Charles lives in the Sacramento, CA area and I had been invited to speak at a conference in Sacramento, CA. During the first meeting with Charles, I discovered that my class ring had two tours in Vietnam: mine in 1967-1968 and Charles' second tour on board an AC-47 Gun Ship in 1971-1972.

If the ring could talk, what a story it would tell!

Chapter Seventeen: Honors And Awards

"Hard work often leads to success. No work seldom does."
Harvey MacKay

On April 3, 1970, one month before the crash, Colonel James Neff, as the Commander, Western Communications Region Headquarters at Hamilton Air Force Base pre-

Colonel James Neff presents George Burk with the Bronze Star Medal, April, 1970.

sented me The Bronze Star Medal. The medal was in recognition of my service in Vietnam from October 1967 to November 1968.

In September 1970, the Air Force Commendation Medal was presented to me by Major General Paul Stoney while I was still in the hospital. General Stoney made a special trip to the hospital to see me and present the award.

The Air Force Outstanding Meritorious Civilian Service Award was presented to me in December 1977 by Major General Robert Sadler. The award was in recognition of my distinguished service as an Air Traffic Control Specialist by applying computer technology to the Air Force air traffic control mission.

The citation reads in part, "Mr. Burk's visionary realization of the potential for computer processing of Terminal Instrument Procedures (TERPS) resulted in an automation program with worldwide application significantly improving the management and accomplishment of this vital function."

In October, 1989, my second wife, Olga, and I were invited to attend ceremonies in Washington, DC, honoring recipients of the *Outstanding Federal Employees with a Disability* awards. The awards are presented annually to federal employees who demonstrate outstanding service to their organizations and communities. All federal government employees world-wide are eligible. Nominations are submitted to the Office of Personnel Management in Washington through the employee's respective governmental agency and are based on ten specific criteria. The nomination criteria include evaluation of job performance, awards received, personal and professional accomplishments and volunteerism.

My journey to our nation's capital to receive the awards was a long and circuitous one, beginning in 1972 while I was a civilian employee with the Air Force. It's important to me that you know the history and chronology of events leading to my nomination.

My nomination to receive the three prestigious awards was initiated while I was a civilian employee with the Marine Corps Reserve Support Command (MCRSC) in Overland Park, Kansas. In August, 1989, my supervisor, Colonel Rex Williams, told me of my selection to receive two of the awards: the *Department of the Navy (DON) Outstanding Employee with a Disability* and the *Department of Defense (DOD) Outstanding Employee with a Disability.*

The awards had been presented annually since 1969, and I was the first Marine Corps civilian employee to receive both the Department of the Navy and the Department of Defense Awards. Although employed with the Marine Corps from October 1983 to March 1994, the nomination criteria covered my entire federal civilian employee service from October 1972 to July 1989. During six of those years, from 1972 to 1977, I was a civilian employee with the Air Force at Richards-Gebaur Air Force Base.

Richards-Gebaur, an early candidate for base closure in 1978, was located thirty-five miles south of Kansas City, Missouri. As an operational military installation, the base served as the Headquarters for the Air Force Communications Command (AFCC). The Commanding General was General Paul Stoney. Richards-Gebaur had an extra special meaning for me as it was the location where General Stoney, Colonel Jim Neff and their staffs arranged for me to re-start my professional career after my medical retirement from the Air Force in October, 1971.

The Navy Award and Department of Defense Award I received were preceded by my being honored as The Outstanding Employee with a Disability, Kansas City Region for 1988. That award served as the inspiration for my nomination by Colonel Williams for the Department of the Navy and Department of Defense awards.

It all began in early July 1989, a few minutes after the morning staff meeting when Colonel Williams, knocking softly on the half-opened door, walked into my office.

"Excuse me, George, do you have a minute to talk?" he asked.

"Sure I do," I replied. "Here or in your office?"

"In my office where we can have more privacy," he replied.

"Hmm," I thought. "Wonder what this is all about. Must be something really important."

I grabbed a pen and a small notebook and made my way to his office. Walking to his office took less than a minute but that gave me enough time to contemplate the reason for the meeting.

I was eager to hear what he wanted to discuss, and perhaps a bit anxious.

Entering his office, I sat in a brown leather chair immediately to the left of his desk, clicked the top of my pen, flipped open my notebook and was prepared to take copious notes.

"How can I help?" I asked.

"George," he said, "I've been thinking about the nominations for the Navy Outstanding Employee with A Disability Award for a week. I've also reviewed the criteria which led to your receiving the Outstanding Handicapped Employee of the Year for the Kansas City Region Award last August."

"Okay, keep talking," I thought. "Are you going to say what I hope you are going to say?"

"The award you received last year was richly deserved," he continued, "So I've decided that I want you to submit your name as our nominee for the Navy Award."

For a few seconds, the office was completely quiet.

"Yes!" I thought. Then I felt a wave of humility.

"Why me?" I asked. "There are other people here who are just as deserving, maybe more so, than I."

"Well," he replied, "after reviewing the award criteria from last year, I don't think anyone else even comes close to you."

"Are you certain," I asked.

"Yes, I am, and I'd like a draft by early next week so I can forward the nomination to Washington to meet their deadline for submission," he replied

"Thanks Colonel," I said, "I really appreciate your confidence in me and the opportunity to receive the award. I'll have the paperwork on your desk within a week."

As I walked out of his office, my mind was a blur. The thought of even being nominated for such a prestigious award made my head spin. My joy, however was mixed with disbelief and was somewhat bittersweet. "Is this really happening to me or is this another dream?" I wondered.

Entering my office, I immediately picked up the phone to call Olga and share the news with her. She was just as surprised and happy as I.

As I hung up the phone, I thought again about the strange path my life had taken since 1970. I reflected about all the people who had helped me arrive at this point in my life. My thoughts about them and the events of my life were refreshing and, yes, a bit painful.

The joy of being nominated was overshadowed once again by the thoughts of the crash and the deaths of my friends. Being nominated for a prestigious award was bittersweet. No honor or award could ever change history and return my friends to their parents, wives and children.

I worked feverishly on the four-page questionnaire and delivered it to Colonel Williams two days later. One week later, in early August 1989, Colonel Williams unexpectedly stopped by my office.

"Your nomination for the Department of the Navy Outstanding Employee with a Disability Award was sent to Headquarters Marine Corps this afternoon," he said. "I think you have a great shot at winning."

"Thanks again, Colonel."

"You're welcome, George," he replied. "You'll be the first to know when I hear anything."

The next few weeks actually went by rather fast. I stayed busy at work so I would not think about the nomination and my chances of being selected. However, my ability to put the award nomination on the back burner soon changed.

On August 29, while sitting in my office reviewing inspection reports, my attention was diverted by a light knock on my half-opened door. Looking up from my desk, I saw Colonel Williams approaching me with a smirk on his face. I stood up to greet him.

"George, I have some news about the nomination," he said

"Hmm," I thought, "I hope I was selected."

"What did you hear?" I asked. I wasn't quite ready for what he said next.

"You have not only been chosen to receive the Department of the Navy *Outstanding Employee with a Disability* award," he said, "but the Department of Defense Award too. Both awards will be presented to you in Washington, DC, in October."

He then explained that all the paperwork approving my selection and official travel to Washington was forthcoming from Headquarters Marine Corps and as soon as he received it, he'd let me know.

We shook hands a second time, he offered his congratulations and walked out of my office.

Two weeks later, while sitting at my desk reading an article on Total Quality Management (TQM), Colonel Williams walked into my office. From his expression, I thought he was going to tell me a story or a joke. I stood up and moved from behind my desk to greet him.

"Congratulations," he said. "Personnel just called me and advised that you have been selected as one of the ten awardees for the Presidential Award for Outstanding Employees with a Disability."

"You're kidding!" I exclaimed.

"No, I'm not kidding," he said emphatically. "Colonel McComb just called me and asked me to convey his congratulations too."

Well, to say I was speechless with yet another good fortune is an understatement, even though those who know me might think it impossible for me to be speechless. I thanked Colonel Williams for his support, we shook hands a second time, and after he left my office, I picked up the phone and called my family and friends to share the good news.

After I completed the calls, the emotion of knowing I would receive another award began washing over me like waves lapping on a beach. I closed my office door, opened my Bible and read Chapter Five of the Book of James. The prophet James writes, "having faith without works is meaningless."

With tears welling in my eyes, my prayer ended by thanking God again for His continued blessings and the opportunities He has given me. Any success I have achieved since my crash, rescue and recovery are because of God's divine guidance. I know He has never abandoned me.

Then, as if on cue, the phone rang. The call was from Jackie Riley, Head of Civilian Personnel, offering her congratulations and telling me that official notification about the awards was forthcoming from Washington.

"The Commandant is sending his personal congratulations in a few days too," she said.

Needless to say, the next few weeks were filled with great anticipation. It's always amazed me how slowly time seems to pass when a person awaits a specific date or when an important event is scheduled to occur.

Viktor Frankl, in his book, *Man's Search For Meaning*, talks about a "provisional existence" related to the quality of his life in the Nazi death camps during World War II. I feel that many of us have experienced this "provisional existence" during our time in the hospital. Interminable days filled the torture of fighting for each breath, the ever-present bitter cold feeling, our skin being scraped, sliced and cut away, and the endless tubes, creams and machines which kept us alive. Later, many of us agreed that a day in the hospital seemed to last longer than a week.

However, there was a "provisional existence" during this time in my life that was totally different. Instead of living from day to day and surgery to surgery, my goal was to travel to Washington to receive the awards. The day to leave just couldn't arrive fast enough.

Finally, the day of our departure for Washington did arrive. While Olga and I were driving to the Kansas City airport, many pictures raced through my mind about the people who played such a vital role in my rescue and recovery. Over the previous eighteen years, I often wondered why my life was spared. What was the larger purpose in my life? How would I know what to do?

"Maybe," I thought, "receiving these awards is part of His plan for me and this is another road I am to travel."

I felt then and still believe today, that the awards I received in 1989 were not just for me but were presented to me as a tribute to all the people who helped me on my physical and emotional journey and as a representative of my friends who died in the crash.

Our week in Washington was hectic but enjoyable. I received the Department of the Navy Award from the Undersecretary of the Navy, the Honorable F. Thomas

Howard. Olga and I attended the presentation in Secretary Howard's office in the Pentagon along with our three escorts. After several pictures were taken, we chatted with Secretary Howard for a few minutes, and knowing he had a busy schedule, excused ourselves to attend a luncheon in the Pentagon's executive dining room.

Commandant of the Marine Corps, General Albert Gray, with George Burk prior to the Presidential Award Ceremony, 1989.

That afternoon in an overflowing Pentagon Auditorium, I was one of ten employees presented the Department of Defense Outstanding Employees with a Disability Award. The awards were presented to us by the Honorable Floyd Spence, Republican Congressmen from South Carolina.

The following evening, Wednesday, October 4, the Disabled American Veterans (DAV), of which I am a life member, hosted a program honoring the ten Presidential Award winners.

The program was held at the DAV's National Headquarters. After a buffet dinner, the awardees gathered on the stage for pictures. A brief biography was read about each of us by the vice-president of the DAV, a former winner himself. Each Presidential awardee was then presented a Cross gold pen and pencil set with the DAV emblem. It was a wonderful evening and set the tone for the Presidential Awards scheduled for presentation the next afternoon in The Department of Commerce Auditorium.

Executive Director, Disabled American Veterans, Head, Office of Personnel Management present a Pen and Pencil Set to George Burk in honor of his Presidential Award for Outstanding Employee with a Disability, 1989.

During our five-day stay in Washington, Thursday, October 5, proved to be the highlight. That was the date ten employees from federal agencies throughout the world were honored with the Presidential Award for Outstanding Employee with a Disability.

The nation's first lady, Barbara Bush, attended the ceremony and presented the awards to each of the ten winners. Mrs. Bush was assisted by Elizabeth Dole, Head of the Department of Commerce, and Constance Berry Newman, Head of the Office of Personnel Management.

The auditorium, with seating to accommodate 2,000 people, was filled to overflowing. Olga was with me, and I was surprised when my sister, Billie Ann Myers, and her husband Jim appeared in the anteroom of the auditorium. They had driven to Washington from their home in Goldsboro, North Carolina specifically to attend the ceremony.

My friend Les Griffin of Mission Hills, Kansas, also was there. Les, enroute to a business meeting in Baltimore, Maryland, rearranged his travel schedule to attend the ceremony. Having my family and friends attend the festivities meant a great deal to me.

Seated on the stage behind a drawn curtain, the awardees, our escorts, Mrs. Bush, Mrs. Dole and Ms. Newman heard the audience talking loudly in anticipation of the ceremonies. I could feel the excitement in the air. To me, it was like attending my first major league baseball game as a young boy or going to the circus. Finally, it was time for the program to begin. As the curtain was slowly drawn, the audience grew quiet and the announcer, in a deep baritone voice, asked all the guests to stand for the presentation of the colors by a joint military color guard. Looking out at a sea of people, trying to find Olga and my sister, I glanced to my left and saw the joint military color guard entering through a side door into the auditorium.

The color guard were impressive in their starched uniforms and added even more pomp and circumstance to the event. It made me proud to be an American! After the national anthem was played, the announcer asked everyone to remain standing to recite the Pledge of Allegiance. Looking into the packed auditorium with the color guard standing erect at the front of the stage, my escort, the Commandant of the Marine Corps, standing behind me to my right, and Mrs. Bush and Mrs. Dole only a few feet away, I lost it!

I started reciting the pledge, "I pledge allegiance to the flag of the United States of America..." then I was overwhelmed with emotion. I couldn't finish the sentence. With tears rolling down my cheeks, I tried to hold my emotions in check.

"Get hold of yourself," I screamed inside.

I lip-synched the remainder of the words, pulled out my handkerchief and dabbed the moisture from my eyes and the tears from my cheeks. As the audience finished reciting the Pledge of Allegiance, I took several deep breaths and sat in my seat on the stage and waited for the official program to begin.

The awards were presented alphabetically, and as each awardee's name was called they moved to the center of the stage, taking a position beside Mrs. Bush. Several of the awardees used wheelchairs and were assisted by a staff member or their escort. A brief biographical sketch was read highlighting the awardee's personal and professional accomplishments. It was obvious to me why these people were selected. I was in good company!

I was the third person called to receive the award. As I made my way to the center of the stage, Constance Berry Newman read my biographical sketch. General Gray accompanied me and stood on my far right, next to Mrs. Bush. Standing to my left were Mrs. Dole and Mrs. Newman.

"We are all honored to be with you here today," Mrs. Bush said as she presented the award.

"I am honored to have this award presented to me by you, ma'am. God bless you and the President, " I said. I also thanked her for taking the time from her busy schedule to be with us.

Mrs. Bush appeared to be truly touched and moved by the awardees and their stories of overcoming adversity through finding purpose in their lives and setting goals and objectives.

Over the years, many people have asked me if Mrs. Bush is as humble and down to earth as she appears on television.

"Yes, even more so," is my usual reply.

General Albert Gray, First Lady Barbara Bush, George Burk, Constance Berry Newman and Elizabeth Dole as George is presented the Presidential Award for Outstanding Employee with a Disability, 1989.

After receiving the plaque, I returned to my seat at the rear of the stage and watched the remaining recipients receive their awards.

Within an hour, the program ended with Mrs. Newman thanking family and guests who attended and Mrs. Bush and Mrs. Dole for their participation. For security reasons, everyone waited until Mrs. Bush and her Secret Service escorts exited the building, then we walked to the anteroom at the rear of the auditorium.

The curtain was drawn as the Color Guard band played John Philip Sousa marches. An unbelievable day was ending for me, my family and the other recipients.

THE WHITE HOUSE
WASHINGTON

Winners of the Presidential Awards for Outstanding
Federal Employees with Disabilities have clearly
demonstrated that disabled men and women are
valuable members of our Nation's work force.
Disabled veterans and other persons with disabilities have a wealth of talent, skill, and enthusiasm
to share with their fellow Americans. They deserve
opportunities within the Federal Government and the
private sector to use their abilities and talents to
the fullest.

I believe that the Federal Government can and
should set an example for all employers. We must
not tolerate discrimination; we should ensure that
employment opportunities are open to all qualified
candidates, regardless of disabling conditions.
As Federal employers, we must take the lead in
guaranteeing respect for the rights and dignity
of disabled Americans.

George Bush

Barbara Bush

Later that afternoon, a luncheon was held at the
Officer's Club at Bolling Air Force Base for the awardees,
their families, guests and escorts. One of the
commemorative gifts presented to each awardee was the
Stars and Stripes which had been flown over the capitol.

144

Then, as fast as it started, all the pomp and circumstance ended! My head was still swimming with all the activity of the previous three days.

I was honored being in the presence of so many fine, outstanding individuals, all of whom had triumphed over life-threatening injuries to become positive influences in their communities and places of employment. The recipients were amputees, quadriplegics, people with hearing and speech impairments, and a plane crash/burn survivor.

The national awards I received over that three-day period were in recognition of my personal and professional achievements before and after the plane crash. Little did I know then that nine years later I would receive another award. This new award was a pinnacle on top of the awards I received in Washington. It was like the cherry on top of a cake.

It was a Wednesday evening, May 13, 1998, when I received a phone call at home from Coach Buck "Guido" Riley, Head Basketball Coach at my alma mater, Adrian College. Olga answered the call in our study and handed the phone to me.

"It's Coach Riley from Adrian College."

I glanced at the clock in the office and noticed it was nine o'clock in the evening Arizona time and midnight in Michigan. My first thought was that someone in the Adrian area or at the college must be ill or he wouldn't be calling me.

"Hi Coach, how are you?"

"I'm fine George," Coach Riley replied. "How are you?"

"I'm good coach. Is everything all right?"

"Yes, everything is okay, George," he said.

"That's good to know. I know it's midnight there. To what do I owe the honor of this phone call?" I asked.

Coach Riley offered his apologies for calling me at that hour. He said that he had called several times earlier but didn't want to leave a message on the answering machine. Given the reason for his call and the good news contained in his message, it was understandable why he wanted to "deliver the message personally."

George," he said, "the Executive Board of the Hall of Fame Committee met last week and asked me to call you. I am pleased to tell you of your selection to the College Athletic Hall of Fame."

"You're kidding, right?" I asked.

"No, I'm not kidding George. In fact, you were elected on the first ballot and that seldom happens."

"The induction ceremonies will occur on Saturday, October 17th during Homecoming Weekend and we all hope you'll be able to join us for this event."

"Coach," I chuckled, "I know you aren't going to believe this, but I'm speechless."

"You're right, George," he said laughing. "I do find that hard to believe."

We both laughed about my "being speechless," then Coach Riley said additional information would be forthcoming in the mail. Several weeks later, I received a letter with details about the ceremony, the names of the other student-athletes to be honored, and the related administrative details. I made our travel arrangements and waited impatiently for the day of our departure from Phoenix to Detroit.

Finally, the big day arrived. On Saturday, October 17, 1998, during Homecoming Weekend festivities, I was formally inducted into the Adrian College Athletic Hall of Fame.

Saturday morning broke with a slight chill in the air and bright sunshine reflecting off gold, purple and red maple leaves. Olga and I left our motel room and drove the five miles to the campus, making certain we arrived in plenty of time before the ten o'clock ceremony. As we entered the large on-campus dining facility where the ceremony was held, Olga and I were met by Coach Riley, his wife Jan, Bill Kenyon, a Vice-president at the college, and several of my friends who live in the Adrian area.

Several of my college classmates, Dr. and Mrs. Harry Speedy of Latrobe, Pennsylvania, and Mr. John Storey of San Diego were there and I was totally surprised by their appearance. They told me that when they read of my induction in the alumni paper, *The Contact*, they changed their personal schedules and just had to "come to Adrian and help honor our old friend." Their appearance at the ceremony meant a great deal to me, and I am honored they were there to share in my award.

After visiting with other friends who gathered to honor me, it was time for the official program to start. The master of ceremonies, Michigan State Senator Jim Berryman, called the function to order and discussed the protocol and reviewed the program. Then, with the head tables leading the way, a morning brunch was served. Dr. John Dawson, President Emeritus of the college, gave the invocation. Dr. Dawson is a man who is loved, admired and revered by many students, alumni, parents and friends of the college in the state of Michigan and around the country. His tenure as president of the college lasted for more than twenty-five years and he was a moving force in its growth, not only in expanding the physical plant, but in raising the college's academic and athletic reputations to even higher standards. During my stay in the hospital, Dr. Dawson sent me several letters which I still have in my possession today. He is a man of great conviction, high integrity, spiritual strength, and a person many of our national leaders could and should emulate. I love and honor him and the others who have helped me on my journey.

After the 156 or so people in attendance finished eating, Senator Berryman introduced Dr. Stanley Caine, the president of Adrian College, who introduced and presented each of the candidates for induction into the athletic hall of fame. After Dr. Caine read a brief biographical sketch of each of the inductees, each honoree approached the dais and was presented an engraved walnut plaque and a special citation from the Michigan State legislature, signed by Senator Jim Berryman. The citation recognized our induction into the college hall of fame and addressed the athletic, educational, personal and professional accomplishments and recognitions each inductee has received.

Inscribed on the brass plate affixed to the front of the plaque, was the person's name, sports played and year of induction into the hall of fame. After Dr. Caine made the presentation, each inductee had the opportunity to talk about memories of Adrian College, and the people and coaches who inspired us. It was our chance to thank all of them for their love and support. A larger plaque honoring each of the inductees hangs in the lobby of the Merillat Sports and Fitness center at the college.

I am honored that I was inducted into my college's athletic hall of fame with men and women who excelled, not only on the athletic field and in the classroom, but in their personal and professional endeavors as well. These other student-athletes whose names will always be a part of Adrian College athletics are Ms. Sue Agosti Kelly of Lakeland, Florida, class of 1986; Mr. Steve Dembowski of Pell City, Alabama, class of 1985; Ms. Nancy Fisher of Tecumseh, Michigan, class of 1967; Coach Jay Flanagan, who was an outstanding coach at Adrian College from 1964 to 1972; and Ms. Nancy Walsh of Adrian, Michigan, another outstanding coach and teacher who coached at the college from 1964 to 1986. The men and women with whom I was privileged to be inducted are a great group of people who have accomplished many great things in their lives and I look forward to seeing them again at the 1999 induction ceremonies.

As the college's final tribute to the newly inducted members of the Adrian College Athletic Hall of Fame, each of us was individually introduced to the crowd before the Homecoming Football game. There we all stood, at the fifty-yard line at the football stadium, receiving the applause and appreciation of family, friends and others gathered on that special day. Then, with a blink of an eye, it was all over!

My only regret is that Mom, Dad, Aunt Anne and other family members who have passed away were not there in person to share this honor with me.

However, I do know my parents, Aunt Anne, Colonel Shelton, Bob Ward, Pappy, Fred Adams, and Kenny Yarger were there in spirit. I still have my angels!

"We're okay, Captain Burk. You need to get better," I often feel as if I can hear Fred saying as clearly as he did before.

I love all of you guys!

Chapter Eighteen: What Does It All Mean?

"If not me, then who? If not now, then when?"
Paraphrase of an ancient Jewish teaching

The thousands of people I've met over the years since the crash have presented me with more questions than answers. People have asked me why I thought my life was spared while the others died. I am often asked, "Do you believe in God?" An almost unanimous sentiment has been, "You have to write a book and tell your story."

I have asked myself many of these same questions over the past twenty-nine years since that fateful May morning in 1970. Heaven only knows, I've had plenty of time to pause and reflect on why I was the only survivor. What does it all mean? Was I really chosen to spread a message of hope and faith to others or was my rescue and recovery merely a set of unique circumstance which just happened?

If I am supposed to share my messages, then "How?" "When?" and "Where?"

I had so many questions and so few answers.

When these thoughts flash across my mind, I often reflect on my first discussion with Dr. Inge in the nurse's break room that afternoon in September, 1970. I can still hear his voice as if it happened yesterday.

"Doc, what am I supposed to do now?" I asked.

And the reply I hear in my mind today is as valid as it was that day, twenty-seven years ago.

"George, you have a purpose. We all have a purpose. It's up to you to find it. No one can do it for you. It probably won't happen as a 'lightning bolt from the sky' but will come to you over time."

"If you want to bad enough," he continued, "you will find that purpose and turn what was negative into a positive. It's up to you."

Well, it is up to me, as it is up to everyone else to find their purpose in life. Every day brings each of us new challenges to learn and grow, accepting the changes around us as opportunities to find out more about ourselves and life!

In *Man's Search For Meaning*, Frankl states, "It's not what we expect from life but what life expects from us."

I know now that suffering is a test of our faith and values that is individual, personal, and different for each of us. In all the world, our suffering is unique; we can choose to see it, use it, and wear it as our badge of honor or we can try to make others feel sorry for us and our plight. There is dignity in suffering and death. We can choose to be survivors or victims. Or we can go beyond survival to take the personal lessons of suffering and the deeper understanding that follows to build on it and turn our survival into success.

My journey since the plane crash has had its share of ups and downs. Fortunately, many more "ups" than "downs." Knowing my life was spared and learning to accept and live with the pain from the burns and internal injuries, I thought that, after that, the emotions of further frustration, anxiety, and fear would be absent from my life.

"After all," I thought, "look what you have been through for God's sake."

During those times when everyday life seemed to get the best of me, I would be overwhelmed with guilt for feeling anxious, depressed, and even angry. Many times, it was a basic human emotion which generated the negative feelings in my mind.

While in the hospital, I convinced myself that these emotions should be absent from my life and if I gave in to any of them, then something must be lacking in me as a man. After all, men are not supposed to cry, right?

Over the years, I have come to acknowledge that, from time to time, I may be overwhelmed with emotions which come from dealing with my physical discomfort.

"Be glad you're alive," I would often scold myself.

"Think of the alternative."

"Life's tough, so what?"

I started to realize that to accept what had happened and to turn a negative into a positive, the acceptance must come from within me. All meaningful change starts from within, and I must be willing to objectively assess my life, my goals and to "start small and start slow."

The Japanese have a quality improvement term called "Kaizen", roughly translated as, "Continuous Incremental Improvement."

Many times while in the hospital and after my release, I felt like the proverbial Humpty Dumpty who fell off the wall. Like the character in the rhyme, I too had all the king's horses and all the king's men trying to put this Humpty Dumpty back together again. My life was like a mosaic which had shattered with the hundreds of pieces lying on the ground. The job of the king's men was to return the pieces on the ground to the appropriate body part. They succeeded!

I also talked to people about my accident while still in the hospital. At a seminar hosted by the burn unit in September, 1970, for religious leaders and medical professionals, I was asked by a local minister to speak at his church on a Sunday morning.

I was reluctant at first but agreed to address his congregation once I was convinced that my appearance wouldn't be treated as some sort of a sideshow. The minister and I agreed that my comments would address the accident, my rescue, and my two near-death experiences.

Not really knowing what to expect, my family and I showed up at the Presbyterian Church just a few blocks from the hospital on the scheduled day and time. We were met at the church by the pastor who handed me the morning's bulletin. There listed as the sermon was, "Baptism By Fire, Captain George Burk."

"Damn," I thought, "I *am* the Sermon."

"What have I gotten myself into?" I wondered. "I hope they like me."

The pews in the large church were filled. It was obvious to me the pastor had done some heavy duty advertising about that Sunday's "preacher". I talked about the crash and the events that surrounded my rescue, and the care I received at the burn unit. My message appeared to be well received as many of the parishioners approached us afterwards and offered their best wishes. Several men and women appeared to have tears in their eyes. I felt really good about sharing my story with them, and I felt I walked a little taller after that day.

I returned to the hospital immediately after my presentation, changed into my hospital pajamas and climbed into bed. I was exhausted!

Dozing off to sleep, I started retracing the many discussions with Dr. Inge, and it began to dawn on me. Dr. Inge was right! My journey will take time, and I needed to learn how to relax and to enjoy the ride.

The emotional lift I received from speaking at the Presbyterian Church in San Antonio really helped me. Looking back, I see it as another turning point in my recovery.

Once again, I could hear Dr. Inge's comments over and over again in my mind.

"We are so busy here, we only have time to heal the body, not the mind," he often said. "When the patients leave here, we don't know what happens to them."

After my release from the hospital, I spoke to various groups in the community in which we lived. Many invitations were extended verbally and only after someone learned the specifics of the crash and my rescue. Speaking to groups was not my focus; getting my

George Burk presents the Keynote Address at the Ontario Professional Firefighter's Association Annual Conference, November 1992.

life back on track was my main purpose and that involved spending time with my family and restarting my career.

When I was asked to address a group, my standard reply about what I charged was, "Buy me lunch."

For the first ten years or so after my release from the hospital, I ate many lunches but never considered myself a professional speaker.

In July, 1988, that all changed when I met Larry Smith of North Richland Hills, Texas at a conference in Tulsa, Oklahoma. Larry was in attendance when I spoke to a group of safety professionals.

"Bubba, you can have an impact on a lot of people," he said afterwards. "You ought to give serious consideration to marketing yourself and speaking to more people."

Later that day, while sitting in my hotel room, it hit me! Larry was sent to me as a gift. He was offering me advice, and it was up to me to do something with his suggestion.

"Ah ha!" I recall thinking, "another 'why' delivered to me by an angel."

Shortly thereafter, my strategy shifted to expanding my expertise as a speaker and trainer. During this period, I attended seminars which addressed leadership, quality improvement and strategic planning. While attending a W. Edwards Deming Seminar in Tyson's Corners, Virginia, in February 1989, several of Dr. Deming's comments hit me right between the eyes. I experienced another revelation. It was as if Dr. Deming were talking directly to me.

In his seminars, Dr. Deming lectured from his book, *Out of the Crisis*. There I was, seated in the back of the ballroom with my boss, Colonel Rex Williams, and several associates, taking notes and listening intently. Dr. Deming began the seminar by reviewing each of his "Fourteen Principles for Quality Improvement," then expanding on each principle as required. His first principle is "Create A Constancy of Purpose." The second, "Adopt The New Philosophy." The eighth is "Drive Out Fear."

Now imagine for a moment that you are sitting in the back row of a hotel ballroom, intently listening to what the "father of quality improvement" is discussing about each of his Fourteen Points for Quality Improvement. Also, try to imagine that you are continuously trying to place your emotions about the crash and your injuries into perspective. It was, and is a continuous, incremental process of improvement.

Suddenly, as Dr. Deming explained points number one, two and eight, I heard the words and knew what they meant.

"Yes," I said aloud, slapping my forehead with the palm of my hand. "That's what I've been trying to do!"

I apparently startled everyone seated nearby because several of them looked at me with doubtful and worried stares, probably thinking I had fallen asleep or lost my grip on reality.

What I heard Dr. Deming say was what I had been attempting to do for eighteen years but couldn't quite put it into perspective. Another gift was given to me in the form of principles for quality improvement to which I could relate. Create a constancy of purpose, adopt a philosophy of personal quality, and drive out fear.

It all seemed so simple now. It was right there in front of me all this time yet I was too dumb or slow to see it. I literally was not seeing the trees for the forest.

"Yes," I thought, "all of the leadership and quality improvement principles discussed at seminars, in books and in the classroom are sequential. They are inside out, not outside in. I must make the commitment to change and ask not if, but how, these and other principles can apply to my personal life."

Eric Allenbaugh, in his book, *Wake Up Calls*, states that "All meaningful change starts from within." The commitment to change begins in earnest when each of us objectively assesses ourselves sequentially—personally, then professionally.

Learning to trust our intuition and knowing that none of us is alone is another of my "lessons learned."

To trust in God's divine love and guidance and have patience in His time is an attribute we must all learn to implement.

We must learn to separate our "wants" from our "needs." What we want is not necessarily what we need and sometimes we need to be careful what we hope for…we might just get it!

I have also learned that self-esteem cannot be taught; self-esteem must be earned and learned not necessarily through our successes but by our errors. It can't be found in a textbook or a classroom.

George Burk presents the keynote address to the New York Firefighter Conference, New York City, May, 1990.

As Thomas Watson Sr., the founder of IBM stated, "If you want to increase your success rate, double your error rate."

Over the years, my thoughts often returned to the times when I wanted to give up and quit. I often thought the best and quickest solution to my misery and the misery suffered by those around me would be to let it end and escape forever the stress and doubt that pervaded my mind. I was tired of aching, itching and just not feeling well and tried to remember what it was like not to hurt and itch. Giving up is the easy part; living is the challenge!

After surviving an event as horrifying as a plane crash, a person could spend some time reviewing every detail of that day to determine if some other safer path or course of action might have been taken. Another course that would alter events; a different decision made to avoid the physical pain and psychological torture of disfigurement that left me wishing, at its worst, that I would die.

If only…What if…?

Well, I didn't die and my life has been full of adventure and excitement. I have been blessed with a second chance, a chance to travel and share my journey with others.

I am now semi-retired, living in Scottsdale, Arizona, and have opportunities to teach part time, travel and speak to various groups around the country.

I am also blessed to have been able to see my three children play sports, graduate from high school and college, get married and have children of their own. Walter, Kimberly and Scott Burk were six, four and two, respectively, the day of the plane crash. I am blessed to have seen them become adults and to see, know and love my six grandchildren: Allie and Jonathan Lais, Tyler and Holly Burk, and Jackie and Walter Burk. Pap-pap loves you "big much."

In his book, *Wake-Up Calls*, Eric Allenbaugh relates the story of a farmer several centuries ago who lost his prize horse.

> "Centuries ago, a farmer began his early morning chores only to discover that his prize horse had run away through a broken fence. A neighbor later said to him, 'It's too bad your prize horse ran away.' The farmer replied, 'Too bad? How do I know the loss of the horse is a bad experience?'

Several days later, the prize horse returned—but not alone. With the horse were nearly a dozen of the finest wild horses that roamed the plains. Seeing the return of the prize horse along with the other horses, the neighbor came over and said to the farmer, 'What good fortune you have experienced!' The farmer again replied, 'Good fortune? How do I know that having all these horses is good fortune?'

The farmer's young adult son, obviously pleased with the new horses, selected one for his own. On his first attempt to ride bareback, the young man was bucked off and broke his leg. Learning of the situation, the neighbor came over and said to the farmer, 'What a terrible experience to have happened to your son.'

The farmer replied, 'Terrible experience? How do I know that the breaking of my son's leg is a terrible experience?'

A week later, a vicious warlord came storming through the countryside, conscripting every able-bodied young man to fight in his bloody battles. The farmer's son was passed over. And so it goes."

We never know when something interpreted as a negative can, over time, turn into a positive. We all receive gifts. It is up to us to accept these gifts as wake-up calls and continue to look for the learning in every situation.

I lost my friends in the plane crash that foggy, rainy Monday morning, May 4, 1970. I honor their memories and friendships and appreciate the many lessons they taught me.

I know my roots and stopped searching long ago for my identity. Although I was not aware of it then, my life took on a new purpose that day while I was lying outside of a burning airplane in the hills near Schellville, California.

Each of us has a purpose in our lives. It is up to us to find that purpose. No one else can or should find it for us. Every day brings new challenges to learn and grow spiritually, personally, and professionally. Remember, it's not what we expect from life but what life expects from us.

As my good friend Larry Smith of Fort Worth often says, "Bubba, every day is an adventure and every meal a banquet." That sums it up pretty well. We are the sum of our choices and how we see the world and those around us.

My journey has been filled with joy, adventure and learning. In my life, I've learned not to expect perfection, but to pursue excellence. I strive to be the best person I can be and to use the skills and talents God gave me. Dick Vermeil, NFL football coach and commentator, has said, "If you don't invest very much, then defeat doesn't hurt very much and winning is not very exciting."

So…we have a choice. We can see life as half-deprived or as continuing to be fulfilled.

I offer you a challenge: when life gives you lemons…make lemonade. Granted, it's not always easy to stay positive. Sometimes it seems it would be easier to just give up and be swallowed up by self-pity.

But giving up is its own punishment.

I will forever remember what Henry Ford said: "Whether you think you can, or think you can't, you're right."

Never give up, never give up, never, never, never give up!

> "Trust in the Lord with all your heart
> and lean not on your own understanding;
> In all your ways acknowledge Him,
> And He will make your paths straight."
> *Proverbs 3:5*

EPILOGUE

As the sole survivor of a plane crash, I've had the opportunity to reflect on my life, its purpose, my personal and professional aspirations and faith. I was incredibly blessed to have survived the crash and thank God for giving me a second life. Every day is a gift. I thank John Davieau who found me and saved my life, Dr. Wellford W. Inge and staff who refused to let me die, and my family and friends who love me.

Since that rainy day in 1970, my life has been a journey toward continuous improvement. Striving for renewed purpose isn't easy. Every day brings new opportunities and challenges to grow personally, professionally and spiritually.

Along the way, I discovered that life is far more than material wealth, status and pleasure. The greatest gift I received besides my health, family and friends, is knowing that there is more. Being able to address groups about my journey and share my vision, mission, goals and objectives is a blessing.

Excellence is the cornerstone of this process and involves my faith—knowing that all I am or will be is provided by a power greater than I. A holistic lifestyle, involving proper diet, exercise and imaging techniques also play a role in this process. The following poem captures the spirit and intent of my messages and, I hope, my life. It is titled, "What Can I Do?"

What Can I Do?

What can I do to make a real difference?

What can I do to know that we're right?

What can I do to help change where we're going?
What can I do to help us take flight?

Give it your all is one of the answers. Hang in and fight may do some good too.

But what is the best thing we could all take part in? What is the best thing we all can do?

Be honest and caring, and use what God gave us. Keep growing and changing that's what we can do.

Be open to changes and help make them happen, look forwards not backwards is something else too.

Be helpful, not hurtful, build up, don't tear down. Reach for the stars, keep our feet on the ground.

Be earnest and trusting, forgive and forget. Love people and work, give more than you get.

Do some of these things and we'll make a difference. Do some of these things and we'll know we are right. Do some of these things and we'll change where we're going, but do all of these things and watch us take flight.

Don't wait for your "wake-up call." With faith, perseverance and commitment, you will receive gifts beyond material wealth. God Bless you!

Captain George Burk can tell his extraordinary story at your next meeting, training session or convention.

For the past twenty-five years, George Burk has served as a college teacher, public speaker and trainer.

College-level courses he has taught include: Aviation Safety, Aircraft Accident Investigation, Strategy and Policy, Total Quality Management (TQM), and Leadership.

His training seminars and workshops follow from what he has learned about the value of life and the importance of personal quality.

His story provides a very personal punctuation to his lessons on total quality management (TQM), safety and fire prevention, and the challenge of continuous quality improvement.

He regularly works with organizations throughout the United States and Canada including: Dow Corning Corporation, Sprint, Illinois Home Builders Association, Texas Firemen and Fire Marshal's Association, The International Airport Rescue and Firefighting Association, New York Firefighter's Burn Center Foundation, British Columbia Fire Chiefs, Adrian College, Ottawa University, CITGO Petroleum, Oshkosh Truck, Pacific Gas & Electric and The Army Corps of Engineers.

Captain Burk also works extensively with schools, has addressed a cancer survivor's association of Humbolt County, California, all of the high schools and three middle schools in Lenawee County Michigan, including Lenawee Christian High School in Adrian, Michigan.

His articles on safety and TQM appear in such periodicals as The Texas Firemen Magazine; The Texas Fire Educators' Magazine; The Quality Magazine, Australia; The International Airport Rescue and Firefighting Newsletter; and the Hospital Fire Marshal's Newsletter.

Some of George Burk's Presentations:

Wake up or Snooze—Your Choice. Getting past your stuff. Exploring life's school which teaches us we are our choices, not our conditions. Creating personal vision and mission with BHAG's—Big, Hairy, Audacious Goals. Plan your dream; work your dream; live your dream.

Establish Accountability—Shape or be Shaped. Anchor your life to a higher ground. Unite the Inside and the outside. All meaningful change starts from within. The transformation from victim to survivor. Dealing with tough life experiences. Making adversity an ally and a tool to learn and grow. Changing the internal script. Turning lemons into lemonade.

Organizational Self-Management. Moving outside our comfort zones and taking risks. Shoveling while the piles are small. You can't steal second base with your foot on first. The six categories of risk and four types of fear. Managers do things right. Leaders do the right things. The Omega leader. Center life on principle, not popularity.

Transforming Your Life Through Change—A Survivor's Strategy. Applying the continuous quality improvement principles: Adopt the New Philosophy; Create A Constancy of Purpose; Drive Out Fear; Add Benchmarking to Personal Endeavors. Explore the strategic paradigms of challenge, commitment, control, confidence, connected. Turn the mirror inwards.

Passing the Salt, Making a Difference. For everyone will be salted with fire. Salt is good; but if the salt becomes unsalty, with what will you make it salty again? Have salt in yourselves and be at peace with one another." Mark 9: 49-50. Create commitment by unpacking your bags. Having the courage of our convictions and willingnes to be vulnerable. How much have you learned, loved, and made this a better place?

Bringing out the Best in Yourself. Principles which foster creativity and innovation. Turning challenges into opportunities. To TEACH: Trust, Empower, Appreciate and Recognize, Communicate, and Have respect for everyone. Analyze: S='s A+B or C; S(2) ='s A+B and C.

Develop an Attitude—A *Safety* Attitude. Your attitude equals your altitude. Connecting our personal vision with purpose and goals. Cultivating self-esteem and creating a balanced life. Using faith and a holistic lifestyle to enhance your personal journey. Humor will get you through anything. Includes examples (slides) which reinforce the importance of following proper safety procedures, equipment utilization, and materials handling.

What People say about George Burk:

"Like you, I believe a person's abilities are far more important than their disabilities. Keep up the good work."

United States Senator Bob Dole

"I was truly moved by your strength, commitment and your ability to convey your powerful message. The impact of your story has stayed with me."

Jack Kreckie, MASSPORT Fire Rescue Department Logan International Airport

"George Burk has made a tremendous impact on the quality of my job and life."

Jill Norris, Director,Sprint Production Control Management Information Services

"Your presentation at the National Society of Executive Fire Officers was incredible and a testimony to the tenacity of the human spirit. Your faith in God, your ability to rise above human tragedy, and your obvious love of life moved me deeply."

Helen Campbell, Exec., Director, Texas Firemen and Fire Marshal's Association

"He was the best speaker we ever had. We've heard the message before, but the way it was delivered was so thought provoking."

Employees, Citizens Gas Company, Adrian, Michigan

"I schedule your presentation last because no one can follow you."

Jimmy Curran, President, New York Fire Fighter's Burn Center Foundation

Contact George Burk:

George Burk
P.O. Box 6392
Scottsdale, AZ 85261-6392
1.800.769.8568
website: http://www.georgeburk.com
E-mail: gburk@georgeburk.com

HOW TO TRAVEL—A Guidebook for Persons with a Disability – Fred Rosen (1997) ISBN 1-888725-05-2, 5½ X 8¼, 120 pp, $9.95 **18-point large print edition** (1998) ISBN 1-888725-17-6 8¼X10½, 120 pp, $19.95

HOW TO TRAVEL in Canada—A Guidebook for A Visitor with a Disability – Fred Rosen (2000) ISBN 1-888725-26-5, 5½X8¼, 180 pp, $14.95 **MacroPrintBooks**™ edition (2001) ISBN 1-888725-30-3 7X8, 16 pt, 200 pp, $19.95

AVOIDING Attendants from HELL: A Practical Guide to Finding, Hiring & Keeping Personal Care Attendants 2nd Edn—June Price, (2001), accessible plastic spiral bind, ISBN 1-888725-72-9 8¼X10½, 125 pp, $16.95, School/library edition (2001) ISBN 1-888725-60-5, 8¼X6½, 200 pp, $18.95

If Blindness Comes – K. Jernigan, Ed. (1996) Strategies for living with visual impairment. 18-point Large type Edition with accessible plastic spiral bind, 8¼X10½, 110 pp, $7 (not eligible for quantity discounts— distributed at cost with permission of the National Federation of the Blind)

The Bridge Never Crossed—A Survivor's Search for Meaning. Captain George A. Burk (1999) The inspiring story of George Burk, lone survivor of a military plane crash, who overcame extensive burn injuries to earn a presidential award and become a highly successful motivational speaker. ISBN 1-888725-16-8, 5½X8¼, 170 pp, illustrated. $16.95 MacroPrintBooks™ Edition (1999) ISBN 1-888725-28-1 $24.95

Value Centered Leadership—A Survivor's Strategy for Personal and Professional Growth—Captain George A. Burk (2003) Principles of Leadership & Total Quality Management applied to all aspects of living. ISBN 1-888725-59-1, 5½X8¼, 120 pp, $16.95

Paul the Peddler or The Fortunes of a Young Street Merchant—Horatio Alger, jr A Classic reprinted in accessible large type, (1998 MacroPrintBooks™ reprint in 24-point type) ISBN 1-888725-02-8, 8¼X10½, 276 pp, $16.95

24-point Gospel—The Big News for Today – The Gospel according to Matthew, Mark, Luke & John (KJV) in 24-point typeType is about 1/3 inch high. Now, people with visual disabilities like macular degeneration can still use this important reference. "Giant print" books are usually 18 pt. or less ISBN 1-888725-11-7, 8¼X10½, 512 pp, $24.95

Buttered Side Down - Short Stories by Edna Ferber (BeachHouse Booksreprint 2000) A classic collection of stories by the beloved author of *Showboat, Giant, and Cimarron*. ISBN 1-888725-43-5, 5½X8¼, 190 pp, $12.95 MacroPrintBooks™ **Edition** (2000) ISBN 1-888725-40-0 7X8¼,16 pt, 240 pp $18.95

The Wisdom of Father Brown—G.K. Chesterton (2000) A Classic collection of detective stories reprinted in accessible 22-point type ISBN 1-888725-27-3 8¼X10½, 276 pp, $18.95

The Four Million: The Gift of the Magi & other favorites. Life in New York City around 1900—O. Henry. MacroPrintBooks™ reprint (2001) ISBN 1-888725-41-9 7X8¼, 16 pt, 270 pp $18.95; ISBN 1-888725-03-6, 8¼X10½, 22 pt, 300pp, $22.95

Bar-20: Hopalong Cassidy's Rustler Roundup—Clarence Mulford (reprint 2000). Classical Western Tale. Not the TV version. ISBN 1-888725-34-6 5½X8¼, 223 pp, $12.95 MacroPrint-Books™ edition ISBN 1-888725-42-7, 8¼X6½, 16 pt, 385pp, $18.95

Nursing Home – Ira Eaton, PhD, (1997) You will be moved and disturbed by this novel. ISBN 1-888725-01-X, 5½X8¼, 300 pp, $12.95 **MacroPrintBooks™ edition** (1999) ISBN 1-888725-23-0, 8¼X10½, 16 pt, 330 pp, $18.95

Perfect Love-A Novel by Mary Harvatich (2000) Love born in an orphanage endures ISBN 1-888725-29-X 5½X8¼, 200 pp, $12.95 **MacroPrintBooks™** edition (2000) ISBN 1-888725-15-X, 8¼X10½, 16 pt, 200 pp, $18.95

Eudora Light™ v 3.0 Manual (Qualcomm 1996) ISBN 1-888725-20-6½, extensively illustrated. 135 pp, 5½ X 8¼, $9.95

The Essential **Simply Speaking Gold** – Susan Fulton, (1998) How to use IBM's popular speech recognition package for dictation rather than keyboarding. Dozens of screen shots and illustrations. ISBN 1-888725-08-7 8¼ X8, 124 pp, $18.95

Begin Dictation *Using ViaVoice Gold* **-2nd Edition**– Susan Fulton, (1999), Covers ViaVoice 98 and other versions of IBM's popular continuous speech recognition package for dictation rather than keyboarding. Over a hundred screen shots and illustrations. ISBN 1-888725-22-2, 8¼X8, 260 pp, $28.95

Tales from the Woods of Wisdom - (book I) - Richard Tichenor (2000) In a spirit someplace between *The Wizard of Oz* and *The Celestine Prophecy*, this is more than a childrens' fable of life in the deep woods. ISBN 1-888725-37-0, 5½X8¼, 185 pp, $16.95 **MacroPrintBooks™** edition (2001) ISBN 1-888725-50-8 6X8¼, 16 pt, 270 pp $24.95

Me and My Shadows—Shadow Puppet Fun for Kids of All Ages - Elizabeth Adams, Revised Edition by Dr. Bud Banis (2000) A thoroughly illustrated guide to the art of shadow puppet entertainment using tools that are always at hand wherever you go. A perfect gift for children and adults. ISBN 1-888725-44-3, 7X8¼, 67 pp, 12.95

MamaSquad! (2001) Hilarious novel by Clarence Wall about what happens when a group of women from a retirement home get tangled up in Army Special Forces. ISBN 1-888725-13-3 5½ X8¼, 200 pp, $14.95 **MacroPrintBooks**™ edition (2001) ISBN 1-888725-14-1 8¼X6½ 16 pt, 300 pp, $24.95

Virginia Mayo—The Best Years of My Life (2002) Autobiography of film star Virginia Mayo as told to LC Van Savage. From her early days in Vaudeville and the Muny in St Louis to the dozens of hit motion pictures, with dozens of photographs. ISBN 1-888725-53-2, 5½ X 8¼, 200 pp, $16.95

Sexually Transmitted Diseases—Symptoms, Diagnosis, Treatment, Prevention-2nd Edition – NIAID Staff, Assembled and Edited by R.J.Banis, PhD, (2003) Teacher friendly --free to copy for education. Illustrated with more than 50 photographs of lesions, ISBN 1-888725-58-3, 8¼X6½, 200 pp, $18.95

The Stress Myth -Serge Doublet, PhD (2000) A thorough examination of the concept that 'stress' is the source of unexplained afflictions. Debunking mysticism, psychologist Serge Doublet reviews the history of other concepts such as 'demons', 'humors', 'hysteria' and 'neurasthenia' that had been placed in this role in the past, and provides an alternative approach for more success in coping with life's challenges. ISBN 1-888725-36-2, 5½X8¼, 280 pp, $24.95

Behind the Desk Workout – Joan Guccione, OTR/C, CHT (1997) ISBN 1-888725-00-1, Reduce risk of injury by exercising regularly at your desk. Over 200 photos and illustrations. (lay-flat spiral) 8¼X10½, 120 pp, $34.95 Paperback edition, (2000) ISBN 1-888725-25-7 $24.95

To Norma Jeane With Love, Jimmie -Jim Dougherty as told to LC Van Savage (2001) ISBN 1-888725-51-6 The sensitive and touching story of Jim Dougherty's teenage bride who later became Marilyn Monroe. Dozens of photographs. "The Marilyn Monroe book of the year!" As seen on TV. 5½X8¼, 200 pp, $16.95 **MacroPrintBooks**™ edition ISBN 1-888725-52-4, 8¼X6½, 16 pt, 290pp, $24.95

Plague Legends: from the Miasmas of Hippocrates to the Microbes of Pasteur-Socrates Litsios D.Sc. (2001) Medical progress from early history through the 19th Century in understanding origins and spread of contagious disease. A thorough but readable and enlightening history of medicine. Illustrated, Bibliography, Index   ISBN 1-888725-33-8, 6¼X8¼, 250pp, $24.95

Rhythm of the Sea --Shari Cohen (2001). Delightful collection of heartwarming stories of life relationships set in the context of oceans and lakes. Shari Cohen is a popular author of Womens' magazine articles and contributor to the *Chicken Soup for the Soul* series.   ISBN   1-888725-55-9,   8X6.5   150   pp, $14.95 **MacroPrintBooks**™ edition (2001) ISBN 1-888725-63-X,   8¼X6½, 16 pt, 250 pp, $24.95

The Job—Eric Whitfield (2001) A story of self-discovery in the context of the death of a grandfather.. A book to read and share in times of change and Grieving. ISBN 1-888725-68-0, 5½ X 8¼, 100   pp, $12.95 **MacroPrintBooks**™ edition   (2001)   ISBN 1-888725-69-9, 8¼X6½, 18 pt, 150 pp, $18.95

Ropes and Saddles—Andy Polson (2001) Cowboy (and other) poems by Andy Polson. Reminiscences of the Wyoming poet. ISBN 1-888725-39-7, 5½ X 8¼, 100 pp, $9.95

Once in a Green Room: A Novel—Keri Baker (2001). After being raped and having an abortion while in college, a young woman struggles to deal with her feelings and is ultimately helped by the insights she gains from her special education students. Contact information for help groups throughout the United States.Part of proceeds contributed to RAINN. ISBN 1-888725-38-9, 5½X8¼, 160 pp, $14.95 **MacroPrintBooks**™ edn (2001) ISBN 1-888725-61-3, 8¼X6½, 16pt, 200 pp, $24.95

Copyright Issues for Librarians, Teachers & Authors–R.J. Banis, PhD, (Ed). 2nd Edn   (2001)   Protecting your rights, respecting others'. Information condensed from the Library of Congress, copyright registration forms. ISBN 1-888725-62-1, 5¼X8¼, 60 pp, booklet. $4.95 postpaid

Inaugural Addresses: Presidents of the United States from George Washington to 2008 -2nd Edition– Robert J. Banis, PhD, CMA, Ed. (2001) Extensively illustrated, includes election statistics, Vice- presidents, principal opponents, Index. coupons for update supplements for the next two elections.   ISBN 1-888725-56-7, 6¼X8¼, 350pp, $18.95

Riverdale Chronicles--Charles F. Rechlin (2003). Life, living and character studies in the setting of the Riverdale Golf Club by Charles F. Rechlin 5½ X 8¼, 100 pp ISBN: 1-888725-84-2 $14.95 **MacroPrintBooks**™ edition (2003) 16 pt. 8¼X6½, 16 pt, 350 pp ISBN: 1-888725-85-0 $24.95

Bloodville -- Don Bullis (2002) Fictional adaptation of the Budville, NM murders by New Mexico crime historian, Don Bullis. 5½ X 8¼, 350 pp ISBN: 1-888725-75-3 $14.95 **MacroPrintBooks**™ edition (2003) 16 pt. 8¼X11 460pp ISBN: 1-888725-76-1 $24.95

The Cut--John Evans (2003). Football, Mystery and Mayhem in a highschool setting by John Evans ISBN: 1-888725-82-6 5½ X 8¼, 100 pp $14.95 **MacroPrintBooks**™ edition (2003) 16 pt. ISBN: 1-888725-83-4 $24.95

The Way It Was-- Nostalgic Tales of Hotrods and Romance Chuck Klein (2003) Series of hotrod stories by author of Circa 1957 in collaboration with noted illustrator Bill Lutz BeachHouse Books edition 5½ X 8¼, 200 pp ISBN: 1-888725-86-9 $14.95 MacroPrintBooks™ edition (2003) 16 pt. 8¼X6½, 350pp ISBN: 1-888725-87-7 $24.95

Growing Up on Route 66 —Michael Lund (2000) ISBN 1-888725-31-1 Coming-of-age novel evoking fond memories of what it was like to grow up alongside "America's Highway" in 20th Century Missouri. (Trade paperback) 5½ X8¼, 260 pp, $14.95 **MacroPrintBooks**™ edition (2001) ISBN 1-888725-45-1 8¼X6½, 16 pt, 330 pp, $24.95

Route 66 Kids —Michael Lund (2002) ISBN 1-888725-70-2 Sequel to *Growing Up on Route 66*, continuing memories of what it was like to grow up alongside "America's Highway" in 20th Century Missouri. (Trade paperback) 5½ X8¼, 270 pp, $14.95 **MacroPrintBooks**™ edition (2001) ISBN 1-888725-71-0 8¼X6½, 16 pt, 350 pp, $24.95

A Left-hander on Route 66--Michael Lund (2003) ISBN 1-888725-88-5. Twenty years after the fact, left-hander Hugh Noone appeals a wrongful conviction that detoured him from "America's Main Street" and put him in jail. But revealing the details of the past and effecting a resolution of his case mean a dramatic rearrangement of his world, including troubled relationships with three women: Linda Roy, Patty Simpson, and Karen Murphy. (Trade paperback) 5½ X8¼, 270 pp, $14.95 MacroPrintBooks™ edition (2002) ISBN 1-888725-89-3 8¼X6½, 16 pt, 350 pp, $24.95

Early Editions Books

Our mission is to expand public access to important information through rapid publication and reprints of timely books and articles. Early Editions Books is an imprint of Science & Humanities Press, but differs from a typical publishing operation as many items may be available early here as prepublication copy, drafts, and U.S. Government reprints for research.

Hardcopy Reprints of Bioterrorism Information

Medical Management of Biological Casualties Handbook with Supplements--US Army Medical Research Institute of Infectious Diseases 4th Edn, (Feb., 2001),A medical management supplement for the basic field manual below. In addition, about 40 pp of supplementary medical information (to October 2001) was added by us on Anthrax, botulism, Pneumonic Plague, Smallpox. perfect bound paperback book 8X 7 160 pp. ISBN 1-888725-77-X $14.95

Emergency Response to Terrorism -A self-study course

(1999) from the US Department of Justice Federal Emergency Management Agency. with quizzes and final exam for NFA Certificate of Completion. Supplementary medical information beyond FEMA content is also added by us on Anthrax, botulism, Pneumonic Plague, Smallpox (to October 2001). 8½X11, 120pp, spiral bound, $14.95

US Armed Forces Field Manual on Treatment of Biological Warfare Agent Casualties. This is the basic manual to which the Medical Management Handbook is a supplement. Supplementary medical information beyond basic content is also added by us on Anthrax, botulism, Pneumonic Plague, Smallpox (to October 2001). 8½X11, 120pp, spiral bound, $14.95.

The Emerging Threat of Bioterrorism--National Symposium on Response to Bioterrorism, Reprint of Vol. 5, No.4 of Emerging Infectious Diseases. Contains historical information on a variety of biological agents of warfare, who has them, observations from small scale and accidental releases, projections of scenarios that could occur if released in the US. Modeling of contagion. 8½X11, 120pp, spiral bound, $14.95

Related books from
Science & Humanities Press

MamaSquad! (2001) Novel by Clarence Wall about what happens when a group of women from a retirement home get tangled up in Army Special Forces. ISBN 1-888725-13-3 5½ X8¼, 200 pp, $14.95

MacroPrintBooks™ edition (2001) ISBN 1-888725-14-1 8¼X6½ 16 pt, 300 pp, $24.95

Read more at mamasquad.com